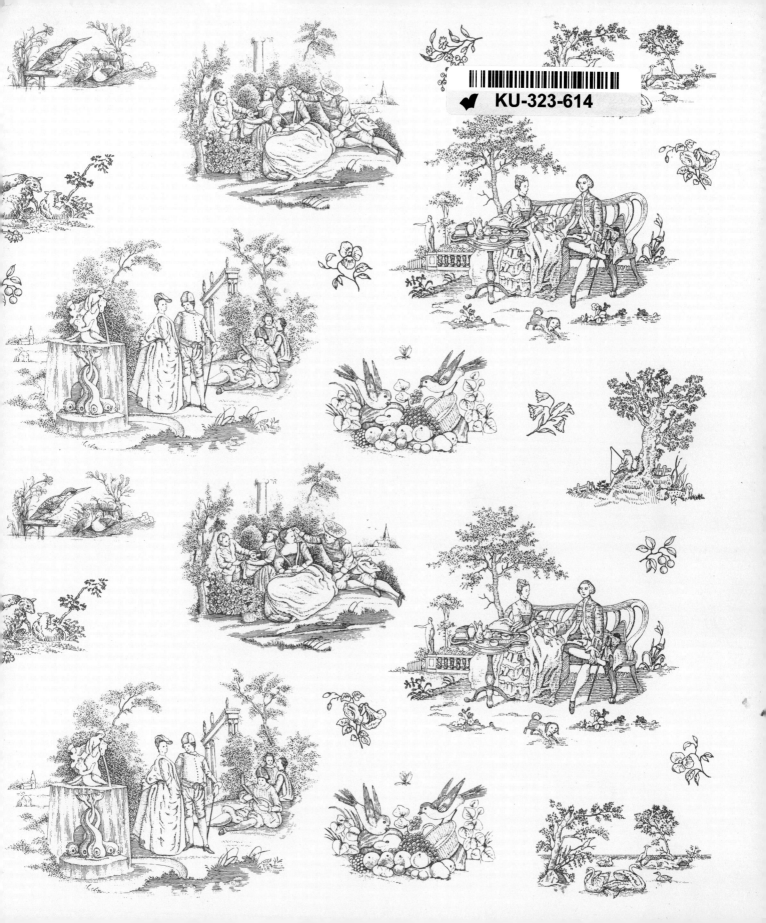

THE FIRST 25 YEARS
of
HALCYON DAYS ENAMELS

Halcyon Days' shop at 14 Brook Street, London W1.

THE FIRST 25 YEARS
of
HALCYON DAYS ENAMELS

The Revival of an English 18th-Century Craft

SUSAN BENJAMIN

 Benjamin Dent

For Bill

who throughout the years
and behind the scenes
has contributed most of all.

End papers: Vignettes after 18th-century engravings.
The designs were adapted to decorate editions of boxes and
clocks produced to celebrate the 25th anniversary
of Halcyon Days Enamels.

Produced by Mandarin Offset Ltd
Printed in Hong Kong

ISBN 0 9505806 1 9

Published by
Benjamin Dent & Co Ltd
23 Bloomsbury Square
London WC1A 2PJ

CONTENTS

Her Majesty Queen Elizabeth The Queen Mother being presented with a box
made in support of the St Paul's Cathedral Appeal by the then Lord Mayor Sir Peter Studd
at a reception on 8th November 1971 at The Mansion House, London.
The box is illustrated on page 134.

ACKNOWLEDGEMENTS

I AM EXTREMELY GRATEFUL to have received permission to reproduce photographs of enamels designed specially for members of the royal family, among them HM The Queen, HRH The Duke of Edinburgh, HM Queen Elizabeth The Queen Mother, TRH The Prince and Princess of Wales, TRH The Duke and Duchess of York, HRH The Princess Royal, TRH The Duke and Duchess of Kent and TRH Prince and Princess Michael of Kent. I would also like to thank HM Queen Noor of Jordan and HSH The Prince of Monaco for their permission to illustrate enamels specially commissioned by them.

In addition I wish to express my thanks to Lady Holland-Martin DBE, Sir Hugh and Lady Bidwell, Mr Mohamed Al Fayed, Mr Bob Smith, Mrs P Cameron Smith and Mr Robert Woodward, as well as those who wish to remain anonymous, for the loan of enamels which are illustrated on these pages. I am also indebted to curators and staff in museums and to others in artistic, charitable and commercial organisations who have allowed me to include the designs specially made for them and whose co-operation has been invaluable.

My special appreciation is extended to Roger Foster, the chairman of Bilston & Battersea Enamels plc, and to all the directors of the company, especially Hugh Gledhill, the managing director, who so generously contributed to the chapter on factory procedures; to Ian Marshall who from the start has administered manufacturing with such commitment and whose advice on techniques has been vital; and to Brent Marshall, who is in charge of production. Additionally my thanks are due to Neal Hughes who, until his retirement, had collaborated with us for many years and who so successfully directed the company's development from the 1970s. I also wish to compliment and thank all the highly skilled men and women at the factory who produce such beautiful objects, and the personnel in administration with whom we work so closely. To Ken and Russell West and their team of silversmiths and metalworkers at Harman Brothers I owe much gratitude for the important part they have played.

I am greatly indebted to my colleagues at Halcyon Days, who have contributed to the realisation of this history of the last twenty-five years and whose total dedication makes each working day so enjoyable, especially to studio director Lia Rose who, since she joined the company in 1970, has been devoted to the revival. To my other co-directors, Maureen Shaw and Delia Doherty, may I extend my profound thanks for their incomparable support over the years. I would like to acknowledge the help given by Noel Riley towards the initial preparation of this book and also to Prudence Cuming Associates for the photography.

Finally and above all, my thanks are due to the collectors of Halcyon Days Enamels without whose loyal support there would be no tale to tell.

Boxes and bibelots dating from c.1770-90,
from Halcyon Days' collection of antique English enamels.

8

HALCYON DAYS opened as an antique shop on 26th June 1950 at 9 Avery Row, behind Claridge's hotel in London's Mayfair. In those days antique shops had a certain formality and most were highly specialised. In contrast, Halcyon Days was set out as a small sitting room with diverse objects grouped together on elegant pieces of furniture. Our stock dated from the 18th and early 19th centuries and included jewellery, clocks, glass, porcelain, silver and Georgian enamels; I used to wonder why all of these articles had continued to be made in various forms throughout the ages, and were still being manufactured, with the sole exception of the enamels to which I was so attached.

Small antique boxes had always attracted me. My mother collected them and because her various finds had fascinated me so much, I frequently went to see the wonderful displays at the Victoria and Albert Museum. The illustrated catalogue of the museum's Schreiber Collection of enamels, published in 1924, has been a major source of inspiration since 1970 when my associates in Bilston and I were able to revive 18th-century English enamels. The introduction to the catalogue taught me that although the generic term for Georgian enamels was 'Battersea', this was a misnomer because the factory was in production for less than three years. It opened in the autumn of 1753 only to close early in 1756 when its founder, Stephen Theodore Janssen, was declared bankrupt and the manufacturing equipment and stock were sold at auction. Thus a very limited number of true Battersea enamels was produced which is why they are so rare.

Other enamelling workshops existed in London but during the second half of the 18th century, the industry's heyday, the majority came from the Midlands. There were many manufacturers in Bilston and nearby Wednesbury, as well as in Birmingham and just one in Liverpool. The impetus that gave enamelling on copper an opportunity to grow into a considerable industry was the development of transfer-printing, an English invention dating from the early 1750s. Although many of the enamels were painted free-hand, transfer-printing enabled multiples of a design to be made and thus it constituted a minor form of mass production. Transfers sometimes provided the only decoration on an enamel but more often they contributed the outline and shading of a design, as a guide to hand painting.

The first enamel boxes met with considerable success in aristocratic circles and this encouraged new manufacturers. Initially their designs were simple and were mostly without borders or ancillary decoration, being painted with flowers, landscapes, harbour scenes, mythological subjects or portraits of famous people. As the industry developed the

A 1950 watercolour by Oscar Almeida of
Halcyon Days' first shop, in Avery Row, London.

enamels became more elaborate and the craft reached its apogee around 1770 with enamels decorated in the most ornate rococo style: colours imitated those of Sèvres porcelain and painted scenes often were framed by scrolling cartouches and diapered backgrounds encrusted with gold or white enamel. Battersea enamels differed from those made elsewhere as they were decorated exclusively with the finest transfer prints in soft monochrome shades; the subjects chosen were usually classical and only occasionally were they overpainted with translucent colours.

Towards the close of the 18th century, as production increased, the quality of enamels began to deteriorate and as they became more commonplace the interest of a fashionable clientele began to wane. But there were other factors that contributed to the general decline, especially of the little box, during the early 1800s. Small patch boxes, for example, with scenes reflecting the life of the period or inscribed with messages of love or friendship, had been among the most popular of 18th-century enamels. Inside each one was a mirror to aid the placing of little black 'beauty spots', devised originally to cover the scars of smallpox but soon adopted as an essential part of every stylish woman's *maquillage*. With the gradual decline of the disease (inoculation was introduced into Britain by Lady Mary Wortley Montagu as early as the 1720s but was not widely practised until later) patches eventually went out of fashion. Once equally in demand were boxes for snuff, in widespread use until the close of the 18th century when the fashion for smoking tobacco began to supersede the habit of snuffing, at least in the best circles. Disruption of exports to Europe during the Napoleonic Wars closed many doors to British goods and a greater awareness of the toxicity of such substances as arsenic and lead (prohibited today) led to a depletion of skilled labour. In addition, the vogue for neoclassicism gradually replaced the extravagances of the rococo style and increasingly the successful exploitation of other materials, such as *papier mâché* and mother-of-pearl, for decorative novelties also played a part in the demise of English enamels – their relative modesty could not compete with the boldness of 19th-century ornamental pieces.

Thus the endearing craft of enamelling on copper, which had so well reflected the sentiments, frivolity and charm of a golden age, came to an end – the last recorded English enameller had ceased manufacturing by 1840. Apart from short-lived revivals, notably by artist-enamellers and jewellers in the late 19th century, the craft remained dormant for the next 130 years.

Above: Two finely painted boxes from the 1770s. *Below:* Early 19th-century boxes with simplistic decoration.

FROM THE BEGINNING the Halcyon Days' shop flourished but during the early sixties, when my two children were small, opportunities for seeking the increasingly specialised antiques in which we dealt were restricted. In those days I had a business partner, Gerda Bram, who later retired, and together we decided to supplement our stock with hand-crafted gifts made to our own designs, either using antique materials or inspired by antique examples. Silver items were among those we commissioned and one day in the autumn of 1968 when discussing new designs with Ken West, managing director of Harman Brothers, Birmingham, I noticed on his desk a small silver bowl with a white interior. On closer examination I discovered it was enamelled and when I asked him where it had been done he told me in Bilston.

This was surprising because comparatively few decorative enamelled objects were being made at the time, although a number of artist-enamellers were creating unique ornamental pieces, usually plaques, on a base of copper, and vast architectural enamel-on-steel murals were a contemporary art form. Also some ceremonial badges and jewels were enamelled on precious metals in the vivid colours that no other medium could provide, and in Scandinavia the technique was developed for modernistic tableware. Otherwise, generally speaking, enamelling was used for refrigerators, cookers, saucepans and similar utilitarian wares.

There were some famous collections of antique English enamels that had been amassed by discerning collectors, notably the late Queen Mary and the Hon Mrs Nellie Ionides, but only limited interest in Georgian enamels existed among the antique buying public. A book entitled *English Painted Enamels* by Therle and Bernard Hughes had been published in 1951 and learned papers and articles on 18th-century English enamels had been written by the two leading experts on the subject, Dr Bernard Watney and the late R J Charleston, Keeper of the Department of Ceramics and Glass at the Victoria and Albert Museum, but it was a comparatively rarefied field.

Thus when Ken West uttered the word 'Bilston' I reacted with great excitement and asked if he would introduce me to whoever enamelled the little bowl. One day in the following December Ken and I paid a visit to a small factory in Meadow Lane, Deepfields, Bilston, where enamel was being produced for domestic equipment. There I met Ken Marshall, the managing director of English Vitreous Enamels Ltd, his son Ian (his younger son Brent joined the company in 1973), his son-in-law Neal Hughes and Tony Wylde, an accomplished local artist who was acting as their consultant and artistic adviser.

Earlier in 1968 Ian Marshall and Neal Hughes had taken over the upper floor of the factory and formed Copper Enamels (Bilston) Ltd, later to become Bilston & Battersea

'All things are sweetened by risk', a box made in 1975; drawings by Rodney Shackell.

11

Enamels Ltd. The purpose of the enterprise was to develop enamelling for use on decorative copper articles. Ian had acquired enamelling skills in 1964 while training at the firm of Jotol in Oslo, Norway. He became and still is works director, while Brent Marshall is production director. Neal's previous technical experience was in engineering and he had also worked in research and development involving the enamelling of heating equipment and domestic appliances. In 1973 the factory moved to Broad Lane, Bilston, and Neal Hughes became managing director; then in 1980 the company relocated to much larger premises at Barton Park, also in Bilston, where it is still situated today. Neal held the post at Barton Park until his retirement in 1993, when Hugh Gledhill was appointed managing director.

And so, to refer back to that memorable meeting in Bilston in 1968, at which there were five men and myself. Until recent years a woman in any sort of executive position in a manufacturing industry was a curiosity and most industrialists were disinclined to discuss business affairs with women, even with their wives. In addition, the north-south divide was a reality – I hailed from London and must have appeared bizarre as I expounded to them my vision of a revival of Georgian enamels.

The firm had been making a range of objects – a napkin ring, an ashtray, candlesticks and a sweet dish among them – enamelled in plain bright colours, in the Scandinavian-influenced style of the time. I learnt that the factory had already executed an order for 1,000 enamel napkin rings and was beginning to experiment with the concept of boxes decorated with transfer prints. I admired the excellence of their finish but I was intent on persuading them of the potential of co-operating with Halcyon Days. I tried to convince them that if, together, we could make Bilston enamels in the 18th-century idiom there would be a market for them. My ideas aroused little or no interest, however, and Ken and I departed in low spirits. Later Neal wrote to say that although he and his colleagues were not interested in a joint venture, if there was something specific I wanted made and was prepared to pay for tooling and prototypes, they would consider it. I replied with an impassioned letter, dropping the names of every celebrated customer of Halcyon Days and painting the rosiest possible picture of an authentic revival of Georgian enamels. They relented, and our two companies began to work together. In due course an agreement was concluded whereby Halcyon Days would design and market the enamels that Bilston & Battersea Enamels would manufacture, each company working exclusively with the other.

In 1970 this small enamel tray featuring Chartwell, home of the late Sir Winston Churchill, won a Council of Industrial Design award in the Historic Houses British Souvenirs competition; drawings by Caroline Ebborn.

A period of enthusiasm mixed with trepidation followed. It transpired that neither company had any spare cash to invest in tooling, and so Neal and I spent day after day visiting Birmingham workshops searching for small metal articles for which the manufacturers already had tools that could be used to press out copper parts for us to enamel. Our first aim was to produce little boxes and eventually we found a small round container that could be adapted as a base for one; it had originally been the salt cellar in a Victorian cruet set. Years later, when various followers and imitators entered the scene, we were amused to note that instead of emulating antique examples they mainly copied early Halcyon Days' concepts and designs. One company issued replicas of our long-discarded, makeshift salt-cellar base, whilst another placed the words 'Bilston & Battersea' as a mark on their enamels as well as in their descriptive leaflets. To distance ourselves from this, in 1980 we changed the brand name of our products from 'Bilston & Battersea Enamels' to 'Halcyon Days Enamels', although the factory retained the former as its company name.

By the late autumn of 1969, after months of discussion and development, we were producing finished samples. Ian and Neal had long mastered the intricate process of enamelling small copper components and I worked with Tony Wylde on design. Several of his drawings were used for the initial range and I began to commission other freelance artists as well. At this stage we had not attempted hand painting, which was to become essential to the realisation of most of our designs.

As weeks passed in frenetic activity between Bilston and London, I began to wonder whether I had been over optimistic regarding the potential of the new enamels. The team in Bilston was devoting much effort towards creating a range of samples and I was putting them to enormous trouble; almost every item produced needed modification or had to be started again from scratch. Would we ever, in just one modest shop, be able to sell enough to justify their efforts and expenditure? We at Halcyon Days thought not and decided that the only fair way to proceed was to arrange distribution to selected retailers.

Two of the leading wholesalers in the gift trade were old acquaintances: Valerie Graham, whose decorative products were made in Italy, and Arthur Kaufman, UK managing director of an American company specialising in silver tableware. Both firms supplied exclusive shops and stores and they readily agreed to show the enamels at the important Gifts Fair at Blackpool in February 1970. The night before they departed for Blackpool, my husband and I gave

Needle case, tape-measure and thimble produced in the 1970s.
Drawings by Caroline Ebborn.

a party at our London flat. Our spirits were high, all of the participants in the enterprise were assembled and we toasted our thrilling new venture with champagne. Little did any of us anticipate the dénouement that was to follow.

Blackpool that February was cold, wet, windy and desolate. The Fair was enormous and widespread, held not only in the Winter Gardens, but also in theatres, garages and ballrooms – anywhere where stands could be erected for the display of merchandise. It transpired that our two representatives' stands were at opposite ends of the town and I spent the entire week at the resort rushing from one to the other, eager for reactions. There were none.

The two exhibitors had been provided with splendid acrylic display notices that announced with a flourish 'The Revival of the 18th-century English Craft of Enamelling on Copper'. We had assembled a range of about thirty pieces, which in fact comprised a few simple message boxes and traditional designs enamelled individually in white, pink or blue. Among the sample objects there was an egg-shaped box, two round boxes, a sweet dish, an ashtray and a little tub to hold cigarettes. Gift buyers from all over the world were there yet not one person asked for a price list or made any enquiry at all.

The embarrassment and humiliation I suffered were beyond description. I had led everyone astray. For the people in Bilston, who had supported the enterprise so generously, and for the two wholesalers who had given the range costly exhibition space, it was a fiasco. To leave it at that was out of the question, but what could be done? Halcyon Days had always sent catalogues to collectors at Christmas time but this was February and Christmas was far away. Although we received occasional editorials in newspapers and magazines, we did not issue press releases. In the absence of any other inspiration, I had a dozen photographs taken and sent them, with the story of our revival, to leading publications.

To our delight during March 1970 we received several good reports in the media and an excellent item appeared in *The Times* on the 19th. On 21st March, however, *The Financial Times* allocated almost half a page to the revival, along with a banner headline 'Bilston & Battersea Bibelots' and

Above: 'I love you today more than yesterday but less than tomorrow' (1972).
Below: A replica of a Chinese 18th-century enamel box in the collection of the Ashmolean Museum, Oxford (1987).

a highly complimentary article by a distinguished journalist, Sheila Black. This outstanding, detailed and illustrated feature caused a stir in both the British and American press. Whole-page articles appeared in glossy magazines and many column inches in newspapers; the *New York Times* and even the *Baltimore Sun* ran lengthy articles relating the history of the decline and renaissance of English enamels. We received hundreds of letters enquiring how the enamels could be ordered but, alas, we had to reply that they could not be ordered, at least not yet.

In the wake of the debacle at Blackpool, the factory was not yet in production: only samples had been made. When we showed our collection at the Fair we realised that if trade buyers had ordered them our forecast for delivery would have been about six months. For a new enterprise, this would have seemed reasonable to the trade but the general public were not used to such long delays. If they read about something of interest, they expected to be able to buy it straight away. So during the following months, while the factory did everything possible to get into production, we wrote hundreds of letters to all who had expressed interest. We explained the sequence of events and gave an assurance that as soon as the factory was ready we would be very happy to supply them with our beautiful enamels. People were intrigued and sympathetic

1980 –

1983 –

1970 – 79

1970 – 73

and this was the beginning of an enduring relationship with our collectors. They understood the situation and many remain customers to this day – indeed some of those original collectors have bought almost every design we have made.

Manufacturing was under way in Bilston by July and we in London were amazed by the ease with which the enamels sold. There had long been a demand from Halcyon Days' customers for gifts of English origin which they could take overseas. They had to be small, not fragile, and cost no more than £10. In those days, prior to the inflationary decades that followed, the majority of our enamels were priced less than this and fitted the bill in every respect. To our astonishment not only were we creating a new generation of collectors' items but we had also discovered the perfect gift.

In August 1970, following the distribution of a small brochure illustrating our new collection, orders flooded in. The demand was so great that we could have sold more enamels than it was possible to produce and this situation continued for many years. As with all things manufactured it was a question of balancing orders and output. But slowly production in this very specialised craft gathered pace; by the 1980s the enamels were being sold by famous shops world-wide and the factory had developed a highly trained team prepared for further expansion. In

All contemporary Bilston enamels are marked.
The two marks shown at the top are currently in use in 1995.

1986 Bilston & Battersea Enamels became a public company.

It was fortuitous that the enterprise had been launched in 1970 as it was a time when people were receptive to what we had to offer. Had the enamels been introduced a decade earlier they might have failed. When future art historians review the second half of the 20th century, they will be bound to comment on the dramatic changes in public taste from decade to decade. In the 1950s, reacting to the utilitarianism of post-war years, decor was flamboyant in homes and restaurants: red velour, ormolu candelabra and gilded cherubs proliferated. 'Cool' and 'functional', however, were the buzz-words of the 1960s when walls were stripped bare and painted white, light bulbs swung from exposed electric flex and Paco Rabanne designed dresses made of aluminium. It was imperative at this period that modish furniture, tableware, ornaments and the like had an austere, contemporary look.

During the 1960s I had worked with several English potteries, among them Hammersley and Crown Staffordshire, which manufactured some of my designs as gift items. Although such firms sustained their markets for traditional wares, it grieved me to see fine bone china being used in its white, undecorated state to produce copies of modern Scandinavian metal dishes and bowls for sale in fashionable shops. But by the 1970s there was a desire for gentler, prettier objects. The increasing influence of leading interior decorators, whose tastes were predominantly classical, resulted in homes with a distinctive period feel and our enamels harmonised perfectly with this more elegant style.

Looking back on the summer of 1950, a few weeks after Halcyon Days' shop opened in Avery Row, we were surprised and delighted to be visited by The Princess Margaret. Avery Row is a narrow passageway between Brook Street and Grosvenor Street and it is unlikely that the shop would have become so firmly established had it not been for the patronage of Her Royal Highness and later other members of the royal family. Not long after the introduction of Halcyon Days Enamels in 1970 we were commissioned by The Queen Mother to design a box depicting Clarence House, her London home. Following this a series of special presentation designs were ordered by The Queen and, subsequently, others by The Duke of Edinburgh and The Prince of Wales. Between 1972 and 1987 we were honoured to be granted their royal warrants as the first ever 'Suppliers of *Objets d'Art*' and one of just ten firms to hold all four royal warrants.

Today in 1995 the international acclaim that the enamels receive must appear to be the result of a studied, long-term marketing strategy, but nothing could be further from the truth. When we started to make contemporary enamels Halcyon Days' principal interest was antiques of many types, but all of us involved in the new venture were fascinated to see whether we could revive an 18th-century craft successfully; none of us, however, remotely envisaged the clamour to buy our enamels that later ensued.

Developments & Distribution

At the outset my colleagues and I agreed that one of the principles of our revival should be to create designs in the idiom of the 18th century, employing drawings by talented contemporary artists rather than to copy the originals. This policy was maintained until we were approached, quite early on, by various museums asking us to produce replicas of Georgian enamels which were in their collections. At first we were wary of the concept of making reproductions. In the 1970s this implied an inferior copy of the genuine article, and was not what we were about. We had embarked on a true revival of a craft and had no desire to drift off course. Under-financed British and American museums, however, had discovered that trading in replicas of precious artifacts could be very profitable. So famous were the institutions initiating these ideas that we overcame our reluctance and today are proud of the replicas and the designs based on museum pieces that we produce. Deciding on which specific museum objects to base new designs is often a lengthy process. Following extensive research we make a variety of suggestions, usually to the curator of the relevant department. Once agreement on this aspect is reached initial rough sketches are submitted, then completed artwork and finally finished enamel samples. If the first samples do not meet with the museum's approval, no matter how slight the adjustments requested, it is always necessary to go back to the artwork stage and to proceed as before. Many curators co-operate enthusiastically in these various stages and find the creation of new enamels inspired by ancient objects a fascinating procedure. The names of the international museums and artistic organisations with which we are associated appear on page 145.

Halcyon Days' shops are acknowledged to hold one of the world's most comprehensive collections of 18th-century English enamels to be found outside a museum, and so in due course it was a natural progression for us to make replicas of some of our own rare antique examples. At Christmas 1993 we introduced the Brook Street Collection, which concentrates on replicas of Georgian enamels and unusual designs that might be of special interest to many of our collectors.

Some of our very earliest successes came

Top: 'Parrots' by Caroline Ebborn (1976). *Left:* A replica of a Georgian box (1977).
Right: A romantic message with a drawing by Anthony Phillips (1973).

17

with the introduction of limited editions. Although special issues are fairly commonplace today, they were comparatively rare in 1970. Our first enamels, decorated with simple subjects such as messages, flowers, birds and so on, were produced in July of that year. So anxious were we to make a success of these that the concept of issuing limited editions had never occurred to us. The idea for the first one came from my son George, a musical ten-year-old who was enthralled by Beethoven. During the summer holiday he suggested commemorating the 200th anniversary of the great composer's birth in 1770 by placing his portrait on an enamel box. Having initially dismissed the idea, we finally took the plunge and announced a limited edition of 1,000 boxes. By attempting a box decorated with a portrait, classical motifs, borders and calligraphy we were entering unknown territory and the

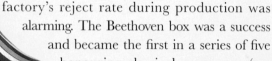

factory's reject rate during production was alarming. The Beethoven box was a success and became the first in a series of five honouring classical composers (see page 76), all in editions of 1,000 which sold out completely.

As well as the limited edition, when a fixed number of items are issued, there is another type of edition known as 'limited production' which is made only for a defined period which is announced in advance. The first limited production edition was a dated egg-shaped box made for Easter 1973. This was greeted with such enthusiasm that we went on to produce series of boxes for Christmas, St Valentine's Day and Mothering Sunday as well as an annual 'Year Box'. For some time now past editions of these have been exchanged between collectors at very many times their original prices; this was a manifestation that simply had not occurred to us at the outset.

The introduction of musical boxes was a development that gave rise to an entirely new series. One day in 1975 Bruce Griffin, a talented designer-engineer, came to Brook Street to enquire whether we might be interested in some small silver boxes he had made and fitted with tiny musical movements by Reuge of Switzerland. We had never sold musical boxes but the miniature scale of his samples had great appeal and I asked him to leave some for us to consider. Later I discussed with Neal Hughes and Ian Marshall the possibility of their producing enamel musical boxes. They

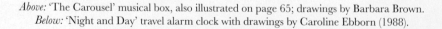

Above: 'The Carousel' musical box, also illustrated on page 65; drawings by Barbara Brown.
Below: 'Night and Day' travel alarm clock with drawings by Caroline Ebborn (1988).

recognised the potential and in spite of all the manufacturing complexities involved in creating such intricate small items in enamel they agreed to work with Bruce. The exercise was wholly successful. Naturally the resonance of small musical boxes does not compare with that of larger ones, but their diminutive size has great charm and they have been much sought after by collectors. Although exceptionally elaborate musical boxes – often incorporated into the cases of clocks and watches – were made in the 18th century, apparently in those days the manufacturers of copper enamels did not realise the potential for developing their ranges of novelties in this respect. Today the scope of the Halcyon Days Enamels collection is being extended with amusing small boxes formed as carousels, birdcages and globes on stands having tiny musical movements fitted into them. We commission many special movements ourselves which play musical extracts ranging from early baroque works to popular Broadway shows.

Our plans for limited editions led to even greater co-operation between the factory and Bruce Griffin. By the early 1980s we had established a rapport with many collectors who took a particular interest in what we were doing. In 1983, therefore, we decided to form a Collectors' Circle with distribution of specific designs only to those who had bought our limited editions in the past and we guaranteed never to advertise them in the press or include them in our general catalogues. The fact that new subjects for the Circle are announced only to a restricted number of collectors gives us, from time to time, the opportunity to develop highly specialised designs and to issue them in very small editions. We wanted something particularly distinctive for our first Collectors' Circle edition and so we set a tiny quartz clock movement, which Bruce had made, into an oval enamel surround. A limited edition of two hundred was announced and they sold out within days (see page 128). Thus we were encouraged to develop a collection of clocks of various types – from traditional 8-day repeater carriage clocks to delicate little table clocks, as well as pendant and travel watches, all incorporating specially designed, hand-painted enamel panels.

One of our most enjoyable activities is the preparation of catalogues which, in addition to a wide variety of newly designed enamels, illustrate the various types of antiques in which

An 8-day carriage clock with drawings by Caroline Ebborn (1980).

we specialise as well as Halcyon Days Porcelain. This latter collection, which originated in 1989, comprises miniature bone china scent bottles, seals and animal sculptures inspired by 18th-century Chelsea porcelain. Created to our designs in a small porcelain factory in Worcester, these meticulously hand-painted collectors' items are in perfect harmony with the enamels.

From the earliest days we exported the enamels to overseas collectors, many of whom regularly visit our shops when they are in the UK. Until 1992 the distribution to retail stockists was administered by Halcyon Days personnel who travelled extensively and exhibited the collection at leading international fairs. In 1992 Bilston & Battersea Enamels took over the trade department and since then all aspects of distribution to retail shops and stores have been judiciously extended by that company. Catalogues are issued by them for use by stockists

and these illustrate the entire range that is currently available to them. Naturally such catalogues exclude Collectors' Circle editions and other specialised designs that are obtainable only from Halcyon Days' shops.

Throughout the revival we have received great support from friends in America. Stanley Marcus, who has bought antiques from us since the 1950s and who was president of Neiman-Marcus in Dallas, has endorsed innumerable designs created especially for the store. Also Roger Horchow, who was vice-president of Neiman-Marcus, has always been a source of encouragement. In 1973 he retired from the store and bought a company called the Kenton Collection (later renamed the Horchow Collection), which at that time owned Cartier in New York. He enthusiastically promoted our enamels and thus contributed further to their popularity with American collectors.

In 1976 The Queen and The Duke of Edinburgh made a state visit to the USA for the celebrations to mark the bicentenary of the American Declaration of Independence. During the visit the *New York Times* reported that Her Majesty had presented President Ford with a special Halcyon Days enamel box as her official

Top: Tiffany's, New York; a box to mark the company's 150th anniversary in 1987. *Left:* Cartier, New York; a box after an Art Deco cigarette case in the company's archives (1977). *Right:* Il Duomo in Florence, made for Armando Poggi (1988).

gift and the President's gift in return was another specially inscribed Halcyon Days enamel box, which had been commissioned from us by Cartier, New York, to mark the occasion.

In the USA the enamels have also been sold for many years by Tiffany's (whose own designs are specially produced), Gumps, Marshall Field, Lucy Zahran, Jacobsons, Scully & Scully and many other stores, shops and museum outlets, all of which succeeded in marketing these quintessentially English *objets d'art*. There are enthusiastic stockists in Europe too, especially in Italy, Germany and Switzerland and throughout the world including the Caribbean, Japan and Australia. Through the years our investigation and development of these markets has taught us that the great appeal the enamels have world-wide is their very 'Englishness'. In the early days, wishing to increase our export trade, we created designs inscribed with simple messages such as 'With Love' or 'Happy Birthday', translated into different languages. These were not at all well received – it was lettering in English that was in demand, regardless of whether or not the message was appropriate or could even be understood. In the UK, in addition to Halcyon Days' own shops, the enamels are also sold by a restricted number of prestigious jewellers and retailers who take pride in promoting our enamels and often stage special presentations of them.

The output of enamels from Bilston has increased at a measured pace and at all times quality rather than quantity has been the main consideration. Our aspirations at Halcyon Days are to continue to make progress by improving the beauty and interest of our designs. My office and studio are in the Brook Street house where the easy communication with the shop downstairs is invaluable. Our mail order and despatch departments are nearby in New Bond Street. In 1984 we opened a City branch in the Royal Exchange, in 1988 a 'shop within a shop' at Harrods, Knightsbridge, and in 1993 another in the celebrated Scottish golfing resort, The Gleneagles Hotel.

Although the boxes have remained the most sought after enamels of all, just as they were in Georgian times, the collection has many other decorative objects and we continue to develop fresh themes, whilst the factory masters new methods to produce them. It has been a stimulating quarter of a century for us all.

Above: A clock commissioned by the Hôtel Ritz, Paris; drawings by Frederick Baylis (1986).
Below: A musical box to mark the 75th anniversary in 1982 of Neiman-Marcus, Dallas; drawings by Shirley Curzon.

COLLECTORS ARE OFTEN curious to know how we decide on subject matter for the Halcyon Days Enamels collection and how the designs evolve. For inspiration we research historic anniversaries endlessly, keep track of current and forthcoming exhibitions, communicate frequently with leading artists and museums, both in the UK and overseas, and trawl through art books and dictionaries of quotations. Collectors themselves often suggest new editions, as do members of staff. My daughter, Laura, has been a constant source of new ideas and witty quotations. Our approach to design has also been greatly influenced by the variety of the 18th-century English enamels in our shops.

Having decided on an idea or an event to be illustrated, I first make a rough pencil sketch to indicate how the elements of the design might be arranged and what further aspects of the subject should be researched. When the appropriate reference material is to hand, a decision is made on what the principal drawing should be and what type of decoration should complement it; such details as cartouches, borders, panels and so on are then considered, as well as the text for the calligrapher. It is only at this point that the studio director Lia Rose and I decide which artist would be most suited to develop each design.

In the Brook Street studio there are five full time artists, the premier one being Christopher Quaile who joined us in 1988 and who was formerly armorial artist at *Debrett's Peerage*. There are also about thirty artists who we commission from time to time on a freelance basis, many of whom have worked for us for over twenty years. There are those, for example, that specialise in architectural subjects, others in landscapes and sometimes several artists contribute their individual talents to a single box. In due course detailed pencil roughs are submitted and these can undergo several alterations as a result of my sketched or written suggestions followed by the artist's amendments, until the artwork is perfected. Artists co-operate with this procedure as they understand the demands made by the miniature scale of the enamels. Eventually when a finished design with all its constituent parts is completed it is reduced

Above: A 'gift-wrapped' enamel box inscribed 'With Love' (1987).
Below: A heart-shaped box with drawings by Zoë Bunker (1994).

in size to fit a specific box or object.

There is no simple explanation for the numbers produced for each edition or for the variation in the shapes and sizes of objects. Diverse circumstances govern our decisions when we are planning a new issue. These include, for example, the number appropriate to an anniversary, production capacity within a certain time-span, or the availability of a particular artist-enameller who excels at painting specific subjects. Although decisions regarding future designs are taken well in advance, the London design team and the factory work so closely together that they can rise to the challenge of preparing an appropriate design for an unanticipated event at comparatively short notice.

At times collectors come to us in search of something specific, such as a design portraying their house, crest or favourite animal. An outstanding example is a box that was made for presentation to a famous industrialist on his 80th birthday; this was decorated on every enamel surface with views that included his five homes, the headquarters of his company and the cathedral where he worshipped. Altogether there were sixteen hand-painted scenes taken from the photographs provided for us to use as reference material. We also receive many commissions from large and small organisations for designs that reflect their activities, portray their headquarters or incorporate their logos.

Above: A design based on the Art Nouveau tiles in Harrods' Food Hall; drawings by Terry Dawes (1989).
Below: The Pre-Raphaelite box with drawings for the outline transfers by Pamela Dowson (1990).

WHILE MANY ANCIENT crafts are barely recognisable today in the guise of modern methods of production, the craft of enamelling on copper has changed surprisingly little. The process of enamel dipping by hand has survived, as have those of transfer application and hand painting. The forming of metal by hand-operated stamping tools was practised before the 18th century and today's power-driven machine pressing for creating copper shapes is but a later version of the procedure. The chemistry and basic preparation of the enamelling ingredients and the repeated firings to build up a smooth enamel coat would be immediately recognised today by a craftsman from the 18th century if he could look over the shoulder of his 20th-century counterpart. Only the use of modern lithographic and silk-screen processes for transfer-printing represents a major change from the time-consuming 18th-century method of engraving the design onto copper plates and preparing the transfers by hand.

This is clearly not the case with ceramics, in some ways a comparable craft. Here old skills are recognisable only in the smaller studios and firms but not at all where manufacturing takes place on a large scale. With enamelling, the methods of the past are not continued just for their own sake. Collectors are captivated by design and quality rather than by the knowledge that old labour-intensive methods are still in use.

Generally, however, the technical progress made has been slower than might have been expected.

The manufacturers of Halcyon Days Enamels employ over two hundred and fifty people who work full or part time. Each enamel item is handled between fifty and one hundred separate times for various processes over a period of about eight weeks before it is finally placed in its presentation case and despatched for sale.

Simply stated, enamels are produced by coating copper shapes with a liquid mixture containing glass, firing them in a kiln to melt the glass so that it fuses to the metal, and then decorating them in the final stage of manufacture. This procedure was followed in the 18th century and it is still in use today. The methods that are described below for the creation of Halcyon Days Enamels focus on the small enamel box which is central to the revival of 18th-century Bilston enamels. The full range, of course, includes a wide selection of clocks, musical boxes, plaques, cuff-links, desk and handbag accessories, to mention only a few.

The process begins with a sheet of pure grade de-oxidised copper imported from smelting factories in Germany which is rolled to a thickness of 0.5mm in preparation for forming. The copper forms are pressed by Harman Brothers, the old-established Birmingham company whose managing director, Ken West, initially played such a vital rôle in the revival; he

The Owl and the Pussycat egg, with drawings by Caroline Ebborn (1992).

retired in 1984 since when his son Russell has been managing director. From the earliest days Harman Brothers have made the vast majority of the copper components and mounts for Halcyon Days Enamels.

Copper shapes, in the form of animals or flowers to be made into boxes known as *bonbonnières*, are created by a London silversmith by the electroforming process; this allows intricate shapes sculpted by a modeller in clay to be reproduced in copper for subsequent enamelling and painting. These unusual, intriguing pieces are a small but distinguished part of the Halcyon Days Enamels range and part of the collection is illustrated on pages 126 and 127.

The mounts, which join together the base and lid of a finished, decorated box, depend on silversmithing, pressing and metal-turning skills. Mounts for round and oval boxes are precision-turned from hollow brass rods and formed into shape; the hinges are stamped out separately – a patented process – soldered into place and then the final assembly is polished and gilded. For the largest sized rectangular boxes, brass strips are drawn through a forming die to render them contoured, the strips are jointed at the corners and then soldered to a hand-crafted, near invisible hinge before they are sent to be polished and gilded.

In the early days of the revival the production of hinged mounts presented the greatest challenge. It was relatively easy to find a jeweller to make them by hand at a prohibitive charge of around £30 each. To produce economic quantities, however, was a problem due to the costly engineering involved. At that stage hundreds were required, not thousands, as the sales potential of the enamels was unknown. The first mounts that were made for us had large projecting flanges and it took some time for the transition from that embryonic form to a more appropriate shape. Eventually sufficient volume was established to warrant our investment in the necessary tooling to manufacture hinged mounts in the traditional 18th-century style.

The basic vitreous enamel has the appearance of small, shattered pieces of glass and is called frit; it is made by mixing together feldspar, titanium, quartz, borax and other inorganic materials. Clay and salts are added to aid suspension of the solids in water and the mixture is milled for up to three hours in a ceramic ball mill to produce a white slurry. Where coloured enamels are needed calcined metal oxides are added to the unground frit and a similar sequence ensues. Before the copper parts can be coated by dipping or spraying – the former for interior and the latter for exterior surfaces – they must be completely degreased and acid-washed to create a clean, roughened surface to which the enamel solution will adhere. The degreasing and etching process has to be completed less than twenty-four hours before the enamelling is begun otherwise grease

The first box mount with its large projecting flange; drawing by Tony Wylde (1969).

contamination from the atmosphere can ruin the preparation.

Great care must be taken to ensure that the enamel coating is even and of the required thickness. Immediately following dipping and spraying the pieces are fired in an electric kiln for approximately seven minutes at around 800°C. This sequence of dipping, spraying and firing forms a basic ground coat and is repeated for subsequent cover coats; usually three to four cycles are required but even a fifth may be needed to achieve the smooth finish essential for the decorating stages that follow.

Much can go wrong during this process, which remains a craft in every sense. The correct depth of coating is vital: too much enamel can result in cracking and too little necessitates further cycles. Kiln temperature is critical, as even relatively small fluctuations due to changes in ambient temperature can spoil the piece. All enamelling on copper involves counter-enamelling, which entails an equal application on both sides. This prevents the metal distorting, causing the enamel surface to crack. Application to the edges is critical: too little edge-covering creates conditions for oxidisation and scale, a frequent cause of rejection in the many subsequent quality checks.

The most vital quality check for every piece occurs directly after the final enamel coat has been fired. It is particularly important to jettison articles which have an inferior finish, poor edges or excess enamel thickness before the decorating process begins. Rejection at this stage is already costly but rejection later for an

Above: The basic ingredient of enamel, called 'frit'. *Centre:* The frit being ground in a ball mill.
Below: Copper components being acid-washed.

undiscovered fault would be much more serious, involving wasted time by skilled decorators.

Decorating is a complex procedure. Initially line drawings for each new design are sent to the factory from Halcyon Days' studio, together with a rough guide to colouring. Preliminary transfers are produced in the factory where, in a small research and development department manned by the most experienced painters, the first samples are decorated. The colouring of a design is rarely completed with fewer than five or six appraisal and repainting stages between factory and studio; the samples travel to and fro by express post accompanied by my detailed notes correcting the application and shading of colours. Occasionally a design is rejected during this exchange and either the artwork is modified or scrapped entirely and started afresh. Only when the finished article is judged to be satisfactory by the London studio is the design finally approved. Master samples, accompanied by detailed briefs, are then prepared by the research and development team, to be distributed later to the painters.

Transfers for the production run are printed by lithographic or silk-screen processes onto transparent yellow varnish-like sheets attached to paper, from which they separate after a brief soaking in water; the 'varnish' burns away in the kiln when the piece is fired. The transfers may provide just the outline of the design, or often contain one or more colours as a background for the later painting by hand. A set of transfers for a box consists of one each for

Above: Dipping copper components into enamel slurry. *Centre:* The transfer library.
Below: Examination of ground-coated components.

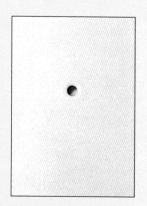 

the outside and inside of the lid, possibly one to go around the sides and another inside, and a Halcyon Days Enamels backstamp to be placed beneath the base, where further information such as the number in a limited edition or the logo of a museum may be included.

The application of the transfer is exacting: correct alignment and the removal of excess water, air bubbles and creases are vital or the enamel will be rejected at the next quality check. Much of the work done at this stage is by outworkers experienced in the craft. They will collect enamels and transfers every three to five days while returning their completed work. A small checking department deals with the administration for this, including piece-work payment for perfect work. While transferring may not have the artistic appeal of hand painting, the skills needed are considerable and take time and training to acquire. Items applied with transfers are dried in a heated cabinet prior to a three-minute firing at 740°C and are then ready to be sent on to the painting department.

Just as the transfer team consists of a group of employees at the factory and a group who work at home, the same applies to painters. In the spring of 1995 there were fifteen trained in-house painters and eighty outworkers decorating Halcyon Days Enamels. A further fourteen trainee painters for the factory team were part of the way through their course, as were nine outworker trainees. In addition to this, many of the painters from the factory team regularly take work home as overtime.

The overall system of outworking involves

Above: A transfer being applied to an egg-shaped box.
Below: Four of the stages in the decoration of the 25th anniversary clock, illustrated on page 144.

a tremendous administrative burden. Once the transfers have been applied to a piece and fired it is taken to an outworker to be painted and then returned to the factory for the next firing. Sometimes the piece may have to be sent back to the painter to have another colour added, and then returned to the factory for yet another firing. This might seem a logistical nightmare, but it ensures the continuing contribution by talented painters who prefer to work in their own homes.

The on-glaze colours required for painting differ from those used for coating enamels as they are the product of extremely finely ground glass combined with calcined metal oxides. The resulting dry powder is blended with a pine oil medium in a machine with triple rollers which produces a very smooth paste. Over forty different colours are produced within the factory in this way. The painters create a palette of up to twenty colours at a time by intermixing the paste colours and diluting them with pine oil to a workable viscosity.

Only very fine brushes of the highest quality are used for the painting process and each painter is trained to decorate a wide range of designs, working initially from a master sample but subsequently from memory. Between five and six hundred different designs are produced each year, but only a few of the most experienced painters tackle the more elaborate, time-consuming items. Some of these are so challenging that they can only be painted in the research and development department. Training lasts a year or more before a painter

Above: Ground-coated components being fired.
Below: Decorated box bases being placed into a kiln.

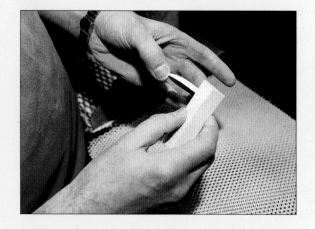

can take her place (men are rare) in the regular team, but under supervision skills and speed continue to develop indefinitely. Initially none of the trainees' work is used for production but gradually they move on to the simpler pieces and eventually to the full range.

Large background areas can be painted over and then stippled with soft tissue to create a textured effect; when dry, the part of the design to be multi-coloured in detail is scraped away and the final painting proceeds. The most complex designs may need multiple firings before they are completed but many require just one three-minute firing at 760°C, which causes the enamel paints to melt and acquire their hard, glossy finish. Occasionally 24-carat gold is added to enhance the more elaborate subjects and the application of gold transfers requires two firings, first at 300°C and finally at 760°C.

All Halcyon Days Enamels are hand painted over transfers, except those that are solely decorated with gold, and certain one-of-a-kind pieces which are painted entirely free-hand. The time taken for even an average sized box is about one hour. Of course the larger, more complex designs can take many hours, even days, of meticulous, highly skilled painting; the decoration of each of the Graham Rust plaques illustrated on page 94, for example, takes approximately fifty hours to paint.

At all manufacturing stages bases and lids of boxes go their separate ways through the enamelling and decorating processes. Only after the last painting firing is the lid and base of a box assembled with its gilded or bronzed brass

Above: Painting the base of a box. *Centre:* A panda *bonbonnière* being painted.
Below: Linishing the edges of an enamel lid.

mount. To ensure a perfect fit the edges are levelled by a procedure known as linishing. In the final assembly, and following careful examination of the components, an adhesive is applied and the boxes are conveyed through a low temperature heat tunnel. The assembly team then carries out a further quality check and is responsible for cleaning and polishing the enamels before they are placed in their dark blue and gold, velvet-lined presentation cases.

The beauty and quality of the enamels and the satisfaction of an artistic skill mastered contribute substantially to the high motivation and loyalty of staff. Long service is normal and there is a remarkably low turnover of personnel. Lynn Jones, for example, joined at the start in 1970 and all of the painters, whether at the factory or freelance, are in her charge. Lynne Owen has been with the company for over twenty-one years; she paints complex designs in the factory's research and development studio and her work is much admired when, from time to time, she demonstrates the skills involved in decorating enamels at special presentations. The premier artist in the research and

development department, Susan Pickford, has been with the company since 1984. Collectors often ask how personnel are found with the necessary skills, but of course they have to be trained and many are recruited straight from school or college.

The planning and supervising of so many different craft processes is a challenge made especially complex by the breadth and variety of the range and the frequent addition of new designs. The procedures involved do not have any of the certainty and reliability of automated mass manufacture. Problems and delays and total rejection of finished items can and often do occur. Enamelling is an imprecise, historic craft, dating back over three thousand years, but the materials and methods used remain unpredictable: perhaps that is why it is so fascinating.

It is interesting to reflect that Bilston is part of an industrial zone, appropriately named the Black Country, and yet over two centuries ago, and once more today, some of the world's most enchanting *objets d'art* emanate from there.

Above: A mount being applied to a finished base.
Below: The final stage: enamels being set into their presentation cases.

POSTSCRIPT

The majority of the enamels illustrated in this book were produced either for special occasions or as limited editions. Some, however, fall into neither category but have been included because their design is of interest. A number of examples are missing, especially from the early days, due to the fact that at the time of going to press I have been unable to locate either the objects or the photographs, and I apologise for these omissions. As well as the editions shown here we have made many hundreds of different designs – from messages, flowers and birds to cartoons and abstract subjects – and my colleagues and I hope that these have brought much pleasure to collectors.

Susan Benjamin

Susan Benjamin

The Halcyon Days legend is inscribed
on a box produced in 1978.
Length of box 2¼" (5.7cm)

ROYAL COMMISSIONS

IT WAS A PRIVILEGE for Halcyon Days Enamels to have received the commissions
illustrated in these pages, for which permission was granted to
draw upon royal archives, emblems and insignia.

The cypher of
The Duke of Edinburgh.
Diameter 2¼" (5.7cm)

The cypher of
Queen Elizabeth II.
Diameter 2¼" (5.7cm)

The Queen's cypher on
an 8-day carriage clock
with painted panels.
Height 3⅞" (9.8cm)

The Queen's coat-of-arms,
the national flowers, and views of
Buckingham Palace, Windsor Castle,
Balmoral Castle and
Sandringham House depicted
on the largest box
in the collection of enamels.
Drawings by Frederick Baylis
and Dennis Flanders.
Length 4¾" (12cm)

The cypher of
Queen Elizabeth
The Queen Mother.
Diameter 2¼" (5.7cm)

Clarence House, a box commissioned in 1974
by Queen Elizabeth The Queen Mother.
Drawing by Ian Adam.
Diameter 2¾" (7cm)

Quartz carriage clock with the cyphers of
The Queen and The Duke of Edinburgh
displayed on the side panels.
Height 3¼" (8.3cm)

The cypher of
The Prince of Wales.
Diameter 2¼" (5.7cm)

Highgrove, the home of
The Prince and Princess of Wales,
commissioned for Christmas 1987.
Length 2⅛" (5.4cm)

The cypher of
The Duke of York.
Diameter 1⅝" (4cm)

The joined cyphers of
The Duke and Duchess
of York.
Diameter 1¼" (3.2cm)

The national flower of Jordan commissioned by
Queen Noor. Drawing by Rodney Shackell.
Length 2¾" (7cm)

Cyphers of The Prince and Princess of Monaco.
Diameter 1¼" (3.2cm)

A *pot-pourri* basket made for
The Princess Anne.
Height 4⅜" (11.5cm)

Nether Lyppiat Manor, the home of
The Prince and Princess Michael of Kent.
Drawing by Rodney Shackell.
Length 2⅛" (5.4cm)

The cypher of The Duchess of Kent.
Diameter 1¾" (4.5cm)

The Prince and Princess of Wales's
visit to Madrid in 1987.
Drawing by Christopher Quaile.
Diameter 1¼" (3.2cm)

The Princess of Wales's
visit to Zimbabwe in 1993.
Drawing by Christopher Quaile.
Diameter 1¼" (3.2cm)

The Prince of Wales's
visit to The Gulf in 1994.
Drawing by Christopher Quaile.
Diameter 1¼" (3.2cm)

An 8-day carriage clock with a
painted enamel panel, made
for The Princess of Wales.
Drawing by Rodney Shackell.
Height 5¾" (14.6cm)

A box designed in the 18th-century
idiom for The Princess of Wales.
Drawing by Rodney Shackell.
Length 2¾"(7cm)

ROYAL EDITIONS

HALCYON DAYS ENAMELS' first box to mark a royal event was designed in 1972, the year of The Queen and The Duke of Edinburgh's silver wedding. This was followed by many other editions produced for royal anniversaries.

In 1993 a replica in miniature of Richard Stone's portrait in oils of The Queen in Garter robes was issued to celebrate the 40th anniversary of the Coronation. The original painting now hangs in Colchester Town Hall.
Length 2⅛" (5.4cm)
Limited edition of 250

The silver wedding anniversary in 1972 of The Queen and The Duke of Edinburgh. Drawing by Anthony Phillips.
Length 2¾" (7cm)
Limited edition of 100

The 30th anniversary in 1983 of The Queen's Coronation. Heraldic emblems of Great Britain decorate the sides. Drawings by Shirley Curzon.
Length 2¼" (5.7cm)
Limited edition of 1,000

The 40th wedding anniversary in 1987 of The Queen and The Duke of Edinburgh. Calligraphy by Frederick Baylis.
Length 2¾" (7cm)
Limited edition of 400

This box celebrating The Queen's Silver Jubilee shows
the State Coach returning to Buckingham Palace
after the Coronation in 1953. The drawings are by
Moira Hoddell whose scenes of Windsor Castle,
Balmoral Castle, the Palace of Holyrood House and
Sandringham House decorate the sides.
Length 2⅞" (7.3cm)
Limited editions of 500 UK and 500 overseas

A beaker was produced in 1977 for
the Diamond Jubilee of the
House of Windsor and the 700th
anniversary of the town of Windsor.
Portraits by Ian Adam; decorative
detail by Frederick Baylis.
Height 3⅞" (9.7cm)

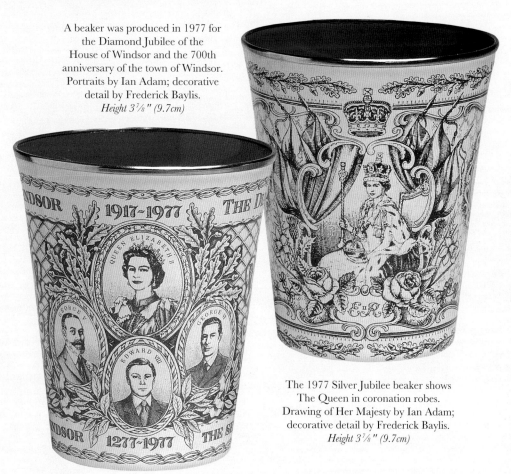

The 1977 Silver Jubilee beaker shows
The Queen in coronation robes.
Drawing of Her Majesty by Ian Adam;
decorative detail by Frederick Baylis.
Height 3⅞" (9.7cm)

The Queen's 60th birthday in 1986 was celebrated with this distinctive drum-shaped box showing Her Majesty at the ceremony of Trooping the Colour of the 1st Battalion, Scots Guards.
Drawings by Arthur Barbosa.
Diameter 2¼" (5.7cm)
Limited edition of 1,000

To mark the 40th anniversary in 1992 of The Queen's accession to the throne. At the time of her accession Her Majesty was staying in Kenya at Treetops Hotel, a vignette of which appears inside.
Drawing by Rodney Shackell.
Length 2⅛" (5.4cm)

The 25th anniversary of the Investiture of The Prince of Wales at Caernarfon Castle on 1st July 1969.
Drawings by Christopher Quaile.
Length 2⅛" (5.4cm)

A box marking the 40th anniversary of the Coronation in 1953.
Drawing by Rodney Shackell.
Diameter 2⅛" (5.4cm)
Limited edition of 500

The Duke of Edinburgh's 60th birthday on 10th June 1981.
Drawing by Dennis Flanders.
Length 2¾" (7cm)
Limited edition of 250

The Queen and The Duke
of Edinburgh's State Visit
to the USA in 1976.
Portrait by Molly Bishop.
Diameter 2¼" (5.7cm)
Limited edition of 200

The first State Visit by
a British sovereign to
Russia since 1908 was
in October 1994.
Drawing by
Christopher Quaile.
Diameter 2⅛" (5.4cm)
Limited edition of 100

The State Visit to Spain
of The Queen and
The Duke of Edinburgh
in 1988.
Length 2⅛" (5.4cm)
Produced for Collectors' Circle
in a limited edition of 500

The Queen and The Duke of Edinburgh's visit to the
Caribbean and Bermuda from 18th February to
10th March 1994. The sides are embellished with the
state arms of the eight countries visited. Drawings by
Christopher Quaile and Fiona Powers.
Length 2⅞" (7.3cm)
Limited edition of 100

The State Visit of The Queen and
The Duke of Edinburgh to the Republic
of South Africa in March 1995.
Drawing by Christopher Quaile.
Diameter 2⅛" (5.4cm)
Limited edition of 100

The Queen Mother's 80th birthday
on 4th August 1980.
Drawing by Caroline Ebborn.
Length 2⅛" (5.4cm)
Limited edition of 1,000

The Queen Mother's 80th birthday.
Her Majesty's portrait, drawn by Rodney Shackell, is
after a photograph by Cecil Beaton, taken in the sunlit
Blue Drawing Room at Buckingham Palace in 1939.
Length 2⅞" (7.3cm) Limited edition of 200

The Queen Mother's
85th birthday in 1985.
Drawings by
Frederick Baylis.
Length 2⅛" (5.4cm)
Limited edition of 2,000

The Queen Mother's 85th birthday. Her Majesty
graciously chose Chopin's *Grande Valse Brillante* from
the ballet *Les Sylphides* for this musical box decorated
with an embossed 'Elizabeth of Glamis' rose.
Drawings by Ceri Evans.
Length 2⅞" (7.3cm) Limited edition of 250

Molly Bishop's 1990 portraits in sanguine
and charcoal of Queen Elizabeth
The Queen Mother appear on these two
90th birthday boxes. The Soldiers', Sailors'
and Airmen's Families Association
benefited from sales.

Diameter 1¾" (4.5cm)

Length 2⅞" (7.3cm)
Limited edition of 500

The wedding of The Prince Andrew
and Miss Sarah Ferguson
on 23rd July 1986.
Drawing by Molly Bishop.
Length 2⅜" (6cm)
Limited edition of 1,000

The wedding of The Princess Anne
and Captain Mark Phillips
on 14th November 1973.
Drawing by Molly Bishop.
Length 2¾" (7cm)
Limited edition of 250

To celebrate the wedding of The Prince of Wales
and Lady Diana Spencer on 29th July 1981.
Molly Bishop's portrait drawings appear on the lid, and
Felix Kelly's views of Buckingham Palace, Caernarfon
Castle, Highgrove and Althorp decorate the sides.
Length 2⅞" (7.3cm) Limited edition of 1,000

Molly Bishop's romantic study appears
on the lid of this box
marking the royal wedding.
Length 2¼" (5.7cm)
Limited edition of 1,500

A memento of the
royal wedding in 1981.
Drawing by Frederick Baylis.
Diameter 1¼" (3.2cm)

A commemorative beaker.
Drawing by Kate Shaw.
Height 3⅝" (9.2cm)

Silhouettes of the royal wedding couple
within a garland of national flowers.
Drawing by Caroline Ebborn.
Length 2⅛" (5.4cm)

To celebrate the birth
of Prince William on
21st June 1982.
Inside the lid is an emblem
of the Welsh dragon.
Drawings by
Frederick Baylis.
Length 2⅜" (6cm)
Limited edition of 1,000

A memento for
Prince William's birth.
Drawings by Frederick Baylis.
Diameter 1¼" (3.2cm)

For the birth of Prince Henry in 1984,
a box with a garland of national flowers.
Drawings by Rodney Shackell.
Length 2¾" (7cm)
Limited edition of 1,000

Pale pink wild roses
decorate an inscribed memento
for Prince Henry's birth.
Drawings by Frederick Baylis.
Diameter 1¼" (3.2cm)

In 1983 the first of Prince William's five birthday boxes was
issued in an annual series of miniatures, progressing in height.
Drawings by Frederick Baylis.
Diameter ⅞" (2.2cm)

BUCKINGHAM PALACE DESIGNS

WHEN THE STATE ROOMS of Buckingham Palace were opened to the public for the first time in 1993, commissions were received to create enamels inspired by the fabulous collections on display.

Right: Carriage clock design after decoration on an 18th-century Sèvres urn. Drawings by Christopher Quaile.
Height 5¾" (14.6cm)

Below: Table clock after an 18th-century astronomical mantel clock by Lépine of Paris. Drawings by Patricia Chitolie.
Height 2½" (6.4cm)

Below : Box inspired by a famous portrait of George IV by Sir Thomas Lawrence. Drawings by Rodney Shackell.
Diameter 1⅝" (4cm)

A box based on the Sèvres porcelain Table of the Grand Commanders of 1806, a gift to George III from Napoleon Bonaparte. Drawings by Rodney Shackell.
Diameter 2⅛" (5.4cm)

The 1977 Christmas Box
with drawings by Moira Hoddell.
Diameter 1⅝" (4cm)

CHRISTMAS LIMITED EDITIONS

THE FIRST DATED Christmas box was introduced in 1971 as a limited edition of 365,
one for each day of the year. The design was inspired by the first Christmas tree
brought to England by Prince Albert and installed at Windsor in 1841,
the year after his marriage to Queen Victoria.

1971

1972

1973

1974

There were twelve boxes in this first
series and in the leap years 1972, 1976
and 1980 the editions each
comprised 366 boxes.
Length 1⅞" (4.8cm).

1975

Until 1975 the mounts for small oval boxes
were of simple construction.
From 1976 onwards they were greatly
improved, being similar in appearance
to those found on 18th-century
English enamel boxes.
Length 2⅛" (5.4cm)

1976

1977

1978

1979

1980

1981

1982

DATED CHRISTMAS BOXES

The NUMBER OF COLLECTORS who wished to buy Christmas boxes exceeded the annual limited editions of 365 to such a degree that a new, dated series was introduced in 1973 and one has been produced every year since. Manufacture of each edition ceases before 31st December of the relevant year.

1973

1974

1975

1976

1977

Diameter 1⅝" (4cm)

1978

1979

1980

1981

1982

1983

1984

1985

1986

1987

1988

The inside of the lids
are decorated with motifs
that complement
the design of the box.
Diameter 1⅜" (4cm)

1989

1992

1990

1991

1993

1994

1995

CHRISTMAS MEDALLIONS

A NEW SERIES was introduced in 1991 in the form of Christmas medallions. Each one is based on a theme of a well-loved carol, a verse of which is incorporated into the design. Every year a limited edition of 365 is produced but as 1992 was a leap year, its edition was increased to 366.

1991
Drawing by Barbara Brown

1993
Drawing by James Ferguson

1992
Drawing by Barbara Brown

1994
Drawing by Barbara Brown

Height of medallions
2⅜" (6cm)

1995
Drawing by Pamela Dowson

53

ST VALENTINE'S DAY BOXES

THE romantic series of St Valentine's Day boxes began in 1974 and each year production ceases at the end of February. Victorian Valentine cards have often been a source of reference for some of these elegant designs.

1974

1975

1979

1976

1978

1977

*Oval boxes, length 1⅞" (4.8cm);
round boxes, diameter 1⅝" (4cm)*

1980

1981

1982

1983

1984

1985

1986

1987

1989

1990

1988

1991

1992

1993

1994

1995

MOTHER'S DAY BOXES

The collection of Mother's Day boxes began in 1975 and each year the manufacture ceases at the end of May. The basket-shaped form of these boxes is based on an 18th-century Bilston enamel design.

1975

1976

1977

1978

1979

1980

1981

1982

1983

Diameter 1⅜" (4cm)

1984

1985

1986

1987

1988

1989

1990

1991

1992

1993

1994

1995

EASTER EGGS

IN GEORGIAN TIMES egg-shaped boxes were among the most appealing enamels made in Bilston; it was a concept that has inspired *objets d'art* through the ages. Each year Halcyon Days Enamels' Easter editions are produced only until the end of April.

1973

1974

1975

1976

1977

Diameter 1⅝" (4cm)

1978

1979

1980   1981   1982

1983   1984

1985   1986   1987

1988

1989

1990

1991

1992

1993

1994

1995

YEAR BOXES

EVERY YEAR SINCE 1977 a dated box has been issued, intended as an individual keepsake and suitable for all kinds of occasions and celebrations especially wedding anniversaries, birthdays and christenings.

The manufacture of Year Boxes ceases each year prior to 31st December.
Length 2⅛"(5.4cm)

1977

1978

1979

1980

1981

1982

1983

1984

1985

1986

1987

1988

Inspiration for the design of Year Boxes is taken from many sources, mainly from the 18th century, and includes English enamel patch-boxes, Chinese watercolours, and silks and embroideries in museum collections. The designs are all based on floral themes and 'A Year to Remember' is inscribed inside the lid of each box.

All dated and limited editions are issued
with Certificates of Authenticity;
these record details relevant to the design
and verify either the final production date
or the precise number in an edition.

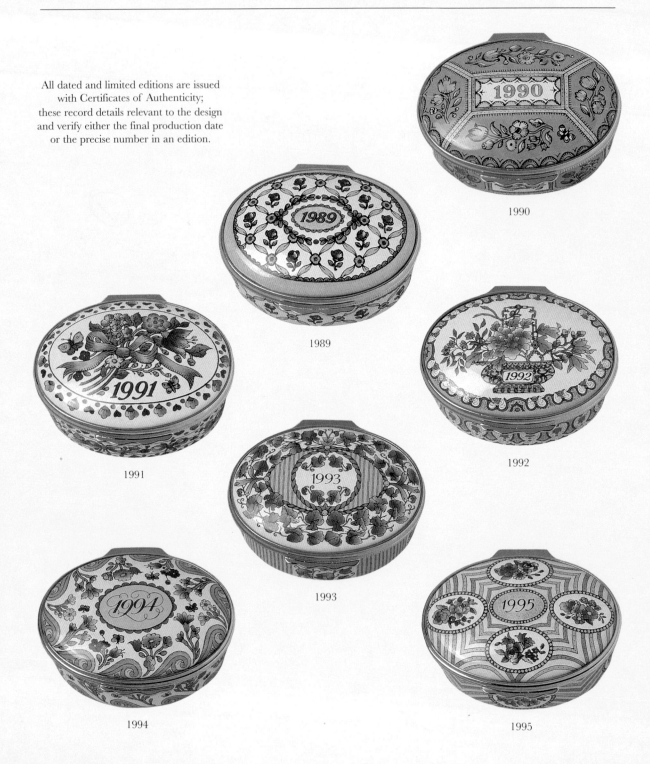

1990

1989

1991

1992

1993

1994

1995

The Carousel Waltz musical box, first produced in 1991.
Drawings by Barbara Brown.
Diameter 1¾" (4.5cm)

WHEN SMALL ENAMEL musical boxes were introduced into the Halcyon Days Enamels range in 1977 the musical extracts were chosen from the past – from classical works, folk-songs and Gilbert & Sullivan. From the mid-1980s tunes from Broadway shows and other popular melodies were added.

A musical trophy for
La Truite by Schubert,
produced in 1977.
Drawing by Frederick Baylis.
Length 2⅛" (5.4cm)
Limited edition of 250

Brahms's *Waltz No 15 in A flat major*, produced in 1978.
Drawings by Caroline Ebborn.
Length 2⅛" (5.4cm)
Limited edition of 750

Le Cygne, the 'cello solo from
Saint-Saëns's *Carnival of the Animals*,
produced in 1979.
Drawings by Moira Hoddell.
Length 2⅛" (5.4cm)
Limited edition of 750

Boccherini's famous *Minuet*,
produced in 1980.
Drawing by Rodney Shackell.
Length 2⅛" (5.4cm)
Limited edition of 750

The *Gypsy Rondo* from Haydn's
Trio in G major, produced in 1981.
Drawing by Rodney Shackell.
Length 2⅛" (5.4cm)
Limited edition of 750

Tchaikovsky's *Piano Concerto No 1*,
produced in 1982.
Drawings by Caroline Ebborn.
Length 2⅛" (5.4cm)
Limited edition of 750

The Royal Shakespeare Theatre in
Stratford-upon-Avon celebrated its centenary
in 1979 and this musical box,
playing *It was a Lover and His Lass*
from *As You Like It*, marked the anniversary.
Drawings by Joyce Hubbard.
Length 2¾" (7cm)
Limited edition of 250

The song *O Mistress Mine*, from Shakespeare's
Twelfth Night, is portrayed on this box issued in 1983.
Drawings by Joyce Hubbard.
Length 2¾" (7cm)
Limited edition of 350

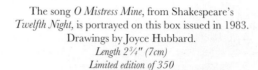

The ball scene from *Die Fledermaus* by
Johann Strauss decorates a box produced in 1982
which plays a phrase from the *Du and Du Waltz*.
Drawings by Moira Hoddell.
Length 2⅞" (7.3cm)
Limited edition of 500

Oranges and Lemons is the musical and visual theme of
this box, issued in 1986 and which plays the traditional
English nursery rhyme. Figures drawn by
Barbara Brown, borders by Caroline Ebborn.
Diameter 2¼" (5.7cm)
Limited edition of 750

Stories from the *Arabian Nights* inspired Rimsky-Korsakov's symphonic suite *Scheherazade* in 1888, later used by Diaghilev for his ballet, first performed in Paris in 1910. This box was produced in 1988. Drawings by Shirley Curzon based on Leon Bakst's original designs.
Diameter 1⅝" (4cm)
Limited edition of 750

A collector telephoned one day in 1980 from Canada and asked whether I knew Purcell's song, *Halcyon Days*, from his music for *The Tempest*. I did not, but bought the score immediately and this musical box was produced. *The Concert Party* on the lid was after an 18th-century engraving by James Basire. Drawing by Frederick Baylis.
Length 2¼" (5.7cm)
Limited edition of 500

An elaborate musical box which plays three melodies: a Mozart *Minuet;* the *Amaryllis Gavotte,* attributed to Louis XIII; and *Serenade* by Hoffstetter. Drawings by Anthony Maynard.
Length 4¾" (12cm) Limited edition of 750

The English ballad *Strawberry Fair* is played by
two of the largest round musical boxes
made by Halcyon Days Enamels.
A drawing of an 18th-century courting
couple by Biz Hull is set within garlands of trailing
strawberry plants by Caroline Ebborn.
Diameter 3" (7.6cm)
Limited edition of 500

William Morris's famous *The Strawberry Thief*
design, painted against a black background,
is adapted to dramatic effect.
Diameter 3" (7.6cm)

69

In 1981 we supported the D'Oyly Carte
Opera Company by issuing a musical box
which plays *Take a Pair of Sparkling Eyes*
from Gilbert & Sullivan's *The Gondoliers*.
Drawings by Barbara Brown.
Length 2¼" (5.7cm)
Limited edition of 1,000

*"The English may not like music,
but they absolutely love the noise it makes."*
Sir Thomas Beecham, 1961

"Rule Britannia" is traditionally played
at the Last Night of the Proms. The Royal
Albert Hall was opened by Queen Victoria in
1871. Since 1941 it has been the home of
the Promenade Concerts which were
founded by Sir Henry Wood.

The Royal Albert Hall
of Arts & Sciences
was opened in 1871 by
Queen Victoria

Diameter 3" (7.6cm)

Diameter 1⅝" (4cm)

The Royal Albert Hall musical box was
produced in 1987, the diminutive version in 1993.
Drawings by Rodney Shackell.

Clara and the Nutcracker,
the painting by
Donald Hamilton Fraser RA,
is depicted on a 1992
musical box which plays
the *Waltz of the Flowers* from
Tchaikovsky's ballet,
The Nutcracker.
Length 2⅛" (5.4cm)
Limited edition of 250

The Royal Ballet's performance
of *The Dream* is evoked in
this box, issued in 1987, showing
Antoinette Sibley and
Anthony Dowell as
Titania and Oberon in
Frederick Ashton's ballet.
Drawings by Shirley Curzon.
Length 2¾" (7cm)
Limited edition of 750

In 1987 we produced a singing bird
musical box with a movement by Reuge of
Switzerland. Drawings by James Ferguson.
Length 4½" (11.5cm)

Barnum and Bailey's Circus
first opened at Olympia,
London, in 1889. The centenary
was celebrated with a musical
box, formed as a circus tent
and playing an extract from
Entry of the Gladiators.
Drawings by Barbara Brown.
Diameter 2¼" (5.7cm)
Limited edition of 750

This box, issued in 1990, plays an extract
from *The Last Time I Saw Paris* by Jerome Kern
from the film *Lady Be Good* (1941).
Drawings by Christopher Quaile.
Length 2¾" (7cm)
Limited edition of 300

In 1986 New York's Metropolitan Opera production
of *Porgy and Bess* inspired this box, which plays
It Ain't Necessarily So. The scenes are based on
designs for the opera by Robert O'Hearn.
Drawings by Barbara Brown.
Length 2¾" (7cm) Limited edition of 750

Zeffirelli's designs for New York's Metropolitan
Opera production of *La Bohème* are recreated on this
box, produced in 1986, which plays
The Soldiers' March from Puccini's opera.
Drawings by Barbara Brown.
Length 2¾" (7cm) Limited edition of 750

A musical birdcage, produced
in 1988, appropriately plays
the song of the bird-catcher,
Papageno, from Mozart's
The Magic Flute.
Drawings by Caroline Ebborn.
Diameter 1⅝" (4cm)

This celestial globe, issued as a musical
box in 1984, is decorated with 24-carat
gold on midnight blue enamel.
Drawings by Frederick Baylis.
Height 3½" (9cm)

Gilbert & Sullivan's *The Yeomen of the Guard*
inspired a colourful box in 1986, illustrated
with scenes based on the D'Oyly Carte Opera
Company's original designs. The musical
movement plays *I Have a Song to Sing O!*
Drawings by Maj Jackson.
Length 2¼" (5.7cm)
Limited edition of 750

Below: The *Petrushka* box, which plays an extract from *Russian Dance*, was issued to mark the centenary in 1982 of Stravinsky's birth. The base design is after Benois's curtain for Diaghilev's 1911 production for the Ballets Russes de Monte Carlo. Drawings by David Walker.
Length 2⅛" (5.4cm)
Limited edition of 750

The Royal Opera House joined us in 1985 to issue this box which plays the aria *Non più andrai* from Mozart's *Le Nozze di Figaro*, first performed in Vienna in 1786. It was based on the designs by Stefanos Lazardis for the 1971 Covent Garden production. Drawings by Shirley Curzon.
Length 2¼" (5.7cm)
Limited edition of 750

In 1985 Dame Margot Fonteyn permitted us to portray her in her role as *The Firebird.* The box plays an extract from Stravinsky's score. Drawing by Shirley Curzon.
Length 2⅛" (5.4cm)
Limited edition of 750

A musical box produced in 1992, which plays an extract from Vivaldi's *The Four Seasons*, composed in Venice. The Venetian scenes depict Santa Maria della Salute on the Grand Canal, the Doge's Palace, the Bacino di San Marco, the Rialto Bridge and Santa Maria Formosa. Drawings by Rodney Shackell.
Length 4¾" (12cm)
Limited edition of 500

To mark the 50th anniversary of Rodgers and Hammerstein's *Oklahoma!*, a musical box which plays *Oh, What a Beautiful Mornin'*, first performed in 1943. The show ran on Broadway for 2,212 performances. Drawings by Barbara Brown.
Length 2⅛" (5.4cm)
Limited edition of 750

The William Walton Foundation commissioned this musical box in 1990 which plays his *Popular Song* from *Façade*. The design is inspired by Edith Sitwell's poems to which the music is set. Drawings by Christopher Quaile.
Length 2¼" (5.7cm)
Limited edition of 75

White Christmas, Irving Berlin's famous song, was first performed in the 1942 film *Holiday Inn* and is one of the most frequently recorded melodies in history. The musical box was produced in 1993. Drawings by Barbara Brown.
Diameter 1⅝" (4cm)

The family of the late Irving Berlin commissioned this musical box in 1994. It plays an extract from *Always*, first performed in 1925. Drawings by Christopher Quaile. Length 2⅛" (5.4cm)

The 60th anniversary in 1984 of George Gershwin's *Rhapsody in Blue*, the orchestral piece composed for Paul Whiteman's jazz concert at the Aeolian Hall, New York, on 12th February 1924. Drawing by Shirley Curzon.
Length 2¾" (7cm) Limited edition of 750

OUR FIRST LIMITED edition was the Beethoven box in 1970. This introduced the Great Classical Composers collection, each box in an edition of 1,000. Mozart and Handel followed in 1971, Bach and Haydn in 1972. The drawings were by Eric Thomas.

'Let it flow from my heart to the heart of all men', from the original manuscript of Beethoven's *Missa Solemnis*, is inscribed inside the box.
Diameter 2¼" (5.7cm)

Haydn, set against a background view of the park at the Esterházy Palace in Hungary where he was Court Musician.
Length 2¾" (7cm)

Inside the lid is a drawing of the house in Brook Street, Mayfair, where Handel spent 36 years of his life.
Length 2¾" (7cm)

Mozart, after the last known portrait of the composer, a drawing by the artist Doris Stock dated 1789. A silhouette of the Mozart family appears inside the box.
Length 2¾" (7cm)

Bach, after a portrait bust by Carl Seffner, dated 1897, in the Paris Opera House.
Diameter 2¼" (5.7 cm)

MUSIC, OPERA & BALLET

THEMES, SETTINGS and costumes from operas and ballets provide superb reference material for creating designs. Our working relationships with some of the great international companies has resulted in many outstanding editions.

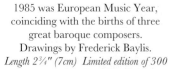

1985 was European Music Year, coinciding with the births of three great baroque composers. Drawings by Frederick Baylis. *Length 2¾" (7cm) Limited edition of 300*

The centenary of Gustav Holst's birth in 1974 was marked with a box illustrating *In the Bleak Midwinter*. Drawings by Moira Hoddell. *Length 1⅞" (4.8cm) Limited edition of 250*

To mark the 25th anniversary of the Aldeburgh Festival. Drawing by Ian Adam. *Length 1⅞" (4.8cm) Limited edition of 250*

A memorial box for Benjamin Britten, produced in 1976. *Length 2⅛" (5.4cm) Limited edition of 250*

To celebrate the centenary in 1976 of the Bach Choir, a woodcut portrait by Gwen Raverat. Part of the proceeds were donated to the Bach Choir. *Length 2⅛" (5.4cm)*

The 250th anniversary in 1991 of the composition of Handel's *Messiah*. The opening bars of the *Hallelujah Chorus* are inscribed inside. Drawing by Rodney Shackell. *Diameter 1¾" (4.5cm) Limited edition of 500*

The Royal Opera House's revival in 1986 of *The Beggar's Opera* by John Gay was marked by a jointly issued box recreating Hogarth's portrayal of Polly Peachum and Lucy Lockitt in Newgate Gaol. Drawing by Rodney Shackell.
Length 2⅜" (6cm)
Limited edition of 250

The ballerina Anna Pavlova made her debut on 28th February 1910 at the Metropolitan Opera House, New York.
Length 2⅛" (5.4cm)

To celebrate its centenary in 1983 The Metropolitan Opera, New York, commissioned the box after Franco Zeffirelli's designs for Verdi's *Otello*. Drawings by Rodney Shackell.
Diameter 1⅝" (4cm)
Limited edition of 750

Scenes from *The Mikado* are captured in the design of this box which marks the centenary in 1984 of Gilbert and Sullivan's comic opera. Drawings by Barbara Brown.
Diameter 1⅝" (4cm)
Limited edition of 740

In 1975 the 150th anniversary of Johann Strauss's birth prompted this box, decorated with a scene of a Viennese ballroom and quotations from *Die Fledermaus* and *The Blue Danube*. Drawings by Moira Hoddell.
Length 2⅞" (7.3cm) Limited edition of 350

To commemorate the 150th anniversary of Sir Arthur Sullivan's birth in 1842, some of the principal characters from the Gilbert and Sullivan operas. Drawings by Barbara Brown.
Diameter 1⅝" (4cm)
Limited edition of 150

In 1981 the centenary of
Richard D'Oyly Carte's
Savoy Theatre, home of
Gilbert & Sullivan opera, was
marked with a box depicting
its famous interior.
Drawing by Barbara Brown.
Length 2⅛" (5.4cm)
Limited edition of 500

The Bolshoi Ballet's visit to
Britain in 1993 was celebrated
with our box featuring the
Bolshoi's principal dancers.
Drawings by Shirley Curzon.
Diameter 1⅝" (4cm)

For the tercentenary of Sadler's
Wells in 1983 our celebration box
depicted Dame Margot Fonteyn
and Sir Robert Helpmann in the
1942 production of the ballet
Comus. Inside there is a miniature
of the original Sadler's Musick
House in Islington.
Drawings by Shirley Curzon.
Diameter 1⅝" (4cm)
Limited edition of 750

A design to commemorate the centenary of the ballet
Swan Lake, to music by Tchaikovsky, first performed
at the Bolshoi Theatre, Moscow, in 1877.
Drawings by Shirley Curzon.
Length 2⅞" (7.3cm)
Limited edition of 500

A tribute to Olivier Messiaen on his
80th birthday in 1988. Inscribed inside
the lid is a phrase of the notated birdsong
from his orchestral work *Chronocromie*.
The RSPB benefited from sales.
Drawing by Suzanne Perrin.
Length 2¼" (5.7cm)
Limited edition of 80

The 50th anniversary of the English National Opera was commemorated in 1981 with this box illustrating some of ENO's outstanding successes: *Boris Godunov*, *The Magic Flute*, *Manon* and *Salome*. Drawings by Paul Kern. *Diameter 1⅝" (4cm)*

For the Royal Ballet's golden jubilee in 1981, a box issued to coincide with the Victoria & Albert Theatre Museum's exhibition, Four Centuries of Ballet Costume. Drawings by Paul Kern. *Diameter 1⅝" (4cm)*

In 1979 the London Symphony Orchestra had its 75th anniversary and this box was issued partly to raise funds for the Anniversary Appeal. Drawings by June Mendoza. *Length 2⅛" (7.3cm)* *Limited edition of 200*

A box depicting interior views of the Opera House and characters from Covent Garden, marked the 250th anniversary in 1982 of the Royal Opera House. Drawings by David Walker.

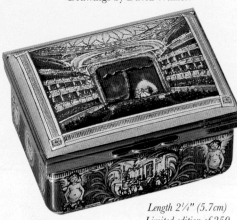

Length 2¼" (5.7cm) *Limited edition of 250*

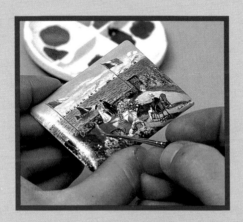

The lid of a box being painted after
La Terrasse à Sainte-Adresse
by Claude Monet,
illustrated on page 83.

81

THE SERIES OF BOXES portraying replicas in miniature of the famous works of great masters are among the most precious we produce. As part of an unusually lengthy painting process, some of the larger boxes receive as many as twenty individual firings.

Young Girl on the Threshold of the Garden at Bellevue by Edouard Manet, painted in 1880; this box was produced in 1979.
Length 2⅞" (7.3cm)
Limited edition of 50

Renoir's *La Danse à la Campagne* was chosen in 1974 for this box, with its green interior, to celebrate the centenary of the first Impressionist Exhibition held in Paris in 1874.
Length 2¾" (7cm)
Limited edition of 250

Child with a Dove (1901) by Picasso, a box issued in 1981 to mark the centenary of his birth.
Length 2⅞" (7.3cm)
Limited edition of 75

Two Dancers on the Stage, painted by Edgar Degas
in 1874, a box produced in 1983.
Length 2⅞" (7.3cm)
Limited edition of 50

The 1981 box in this series was after
The Seine at Marly by Camille Pissarro,
painted in 1871.
Length 2⅞" (7.3cm)
Limited edition of 50

The centenary in 1984 of Modigliani's birth
was marked by a box decorated after
his *Landscape at Cagnes*, painted in 1919.
Length 2⅞" (7.3cm)
Limited edition of 50

Claude Monet's *La Terrasse à Sainte-Adresse*,
painted in 1866, a box issued in 1982.
Length 2⅞" (7.3cm)
Limited edition of 50

A series of smaller rectangular boxes was introduced in 1985 with Cézanne's *Blue Vase* (1885-87).
Length 2⅜" (6cm)
Limited edition of 250

Pissarro's *Pink Peonies* (1873) was produced in 1986.
Length 2⅜" (6cm)
Limited edition of 250

The box featuring Renoir's *La Première Sortie*, which is in the National Gallery, London, was produced in 1985. Renoir painted the work in 1875-76 and it typified his interest in figural subjects over the landscapes and still lives that preoccupied the other Impressionists.
Length 2⅞" (7.3cm)
Limited edition of 50

John Singer Sargent's view of *Claude Monet Painting at the Edge of a Wood*. Sargent was an adherent of the Impressionists, if not one of them. He greatly admired Monet and had bought one of his works at the time this scene was painted at Giverny in 1888. This box was produced in 1986.
Length 2⅞" (7.3cm) Limited edition of 50

Manet's *Roses and a Tulip in a*
Glass Vase (1882), produced in 1987.
Length 2⅜" (6cm)
Limited edition of 250

Peonies in a Vase (1864-65), also
by Manet, produced in 1988.
Length 2⅜" (6cm)
Limited edition of 250

Rousseau's *Flowers in a Vase*
(1909), produced in 1989.
Length 2⅜" (6cm)
Limited edition of 250

J M W Turner's watercolour vignette of
Traitor's Gate, Tower of London (1832), which exemplifies
his superb architectural draughtsmanship, is one of a
group of watercolours, now in the Turner Collection
at The Tate Gallery; they were designed by
the artist to be engraved as illustrations for
books of poetry. The box was produced in 1987.
Length 2⅞" (7.3cm) Limited edition of 75

A Cornfield with Cypresses by Van Gogh, now in the
National Gallery, London, was originally painted in
October 1889 while the artist was at the asylum in
Saint-Rémy. To mark the centenary this miniature
representation was produced in 1989.
Length 2⅞" (7.3cm)
Limited edition of 75

Fantin-Latour's
White Roses in a Glass Vase (1875),
was produced as a box in 1990.
The painting is in the collection
of the Guildhall Art Gallery
in the City of London, and this
edition was commissioned by the
then Lord Mayor of London,
Sir Hugh Bidwell.
The Lord Mayor's charities
received part of the proceeds
from the sale of this box.
Diameter 1¾"(4.5cm)
Limited edition of 500

Pissarro's *Bouquet of Flowers*
(1873), a box produced in 1993.
Diameter 1¾"(4.5cm)
Limited edition of 250

The White Horse by Gauguin (1898),
a box produced in 1989.
Length 2⅞" (7.3cm)
Limited edition of 75

Cézanne's *Still Life with Apples & Oranges* (c.1895)
was the subject of the 1990 box.
Length 2⅞" (7.3cm)
Limited edition of 75

Berthe Morisot's *Chasing Butterflies* (1874),
a box produced in 1991.
Length 2⅞" (7.3cm)
Limited edition of 75

Boudin's *The Jetty at
the Mouth of the Grand
Canal, Venice* (1895),
a box produced in 1992.
*Length 2⅞" (7.3cm)
Limited edition of 75*

La Goulue at the Moulin Rouge (1891)
was the first of Toulouse-Lautrec's
famous posters to be published;
we marked its centenary in 1991.
*Length 2⅜" (6cm)
Limited edition of 250*

Sisley's *Wheatfields near
Argenteuil* (1873),
a box produced in 1993.
*Length 2⅞" (7.3cm)
Limited edition of 75*

*Tropical Storm with a
Tiger (Surpris!)*
by Henri Rousseau,
painted in 1891, was the
1994 box in the series.
*Length 2⅞" (7.3cm)
Limited edition of 75*

Gauguin's *Mandolin and Flowers* (1885),
a box produced in 1992.
*Length 2⅜" (6cm)
Limited edition of 250*

IN ASSOCIATION WITH the Royal Academy of Arts, London, a series was initiated featuring the work of past and present Royal Academicians. Some of the subjects are after existing paintings but many have been created especially for the enamels.

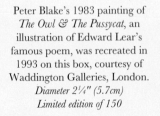

Peter Blake's 1983 painting of *The Owl & The Pussycat*, an illustration of Edward Lear's famous poem, was recreated in 1993 on this box, courtesy of Waddington Galleries, London.
Diameter 2¼" (5.7cm)
Limited edition of 150

Below: Peter Blake exhibited his watercolour *Flowers in a Vase* or *A Posy for Liberty* in 1983 at the Tate Gallery; he kindly gave permission for us to reproduce it on an enamel plaque in 1991.
Height 5¾" (14.6cm)
Limited edition of 75

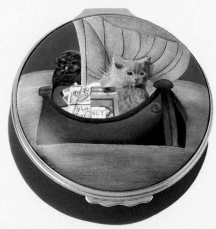

Peter Blake painted *Mabel Stark, the 80-year-old Lion Tamer* in 1961. The box was produced in 1983.
Length 2¼" (5.7cm) Limited edition of 100

Donald Hamilton Fraser's *Poinsettia*, painted especially for this box, produced in 1979.
Diameter 2¼" (5.7cm) Limited edition of 100

As a tribute to Sir Hugh Casson upon
his retirement in 1984 after eight years
as President of the Royal Academy, a
box with his watercolour, *Sailing*.
Diameter 2¼" (5.7cm)
Limited edition of 200

A box specially designed by John Ward, inscribed inside
with a quotation from Sir Joshua Reynolds: 'If you have
great talents, industry will improve them; if you have but
moderate abilities industry will supply their deficiency'.
Length 2¾" (7cm) Limited edition of 200

A spill vase, produced in 1986 after a design
by John Yenn, one of the RA's
first students in 1769.
Height 3⅜" (8.5cm) Limited edition of 250

Leonard Rosoman created *Cat in a Window* in
1991 especially for this enamel plaque.
Height 5¾" (14.6cm) Limited edition of 75

A detail from
November Roses,
a 1984 oil painting by
Sir Robin Philipson
PPRA (d.1992), a box
produced in 1994.
Diameter 1⅝" (4cm)
Limited edition of 100

Ben Levene's watercolour *Fruit Bowl*
(1979), a box produced in 1982.
Length 2¼" (5.7cm)
Limited edition of 500

Frederick Gore's rendering of
Hibiscus on a Covered Terrace, July,
painted in 1990, was
issued as a box in 1992.
Diameter 1⅝" (4cm)
Limited edition of 100

A detail from
Elizabeth
Blackadder's
1992 painting,
Cats and Gladioli,
produced in 1993.
Diameter 1¼" (3.2cm)

Diana Armfield's *Autumn
Flowers from the Garden* (1983),
produced as a box in 1993,
courtesy of Browse & Darby.
Length 2⅛" (5.4cm)
Limited edition of 100

George Stubbs's *Self-Portrait on a Grey
Hunter* (1782), a box produced in 1992.
The original, enamelled on a Wedgwood
jasper plaque, is in the Lady Lever Art
Gallery, Port Sunlight, Liverpool.
Length 2¼" (5.7cm) Limited edition of 250

The Casino, Monte Carlo,
after a watercolour by
Paul Hogarth from a collection
prepared for the book
Graham Greene Country,
published in 1986 in
collaboration with the author;
the box was produced in 1992.
Diameter 2¼" (5.7cm)

In 1992 Sir Hugh Casson PPRA
paid tribute to the memory of
Sir Joshua Reynolds, the first
President of the Royal
Academy, with this
drawing to mark the
bicentenary of his death.
Length 2⅛" (5.4cm)
Limited edition of 200

San Giorgio Maggiore, Venice, after a
watercolour by Sir Hugh Casson PPRA,
was issued to coincide with
'The Genius of Venice 1500-1600'
exhibition at the Royal Academy in 1983-84.
Length 2⅛" (5.4cm) Limited edition of 500

Donald Hamilton Fraser's 1984 paintings of *Petrouchka*
and *The Ballerina*, from the ballet *Petrouchka*, are the images
on this pair of enamel plaques, issued in 1992.
Height 7½" (19cm) Limited edition of 25 pairs

20TH-CENTURY ARTISTS

THE VIVID COLOURS of enamels can faithfully reproduce designs by contemporary artists whose works have brought a refreshing boldness into the collection.

In 1975, 1976 and 1977 we produced a trio
of boxes after designs by Fleur Cowles.
Diameter 2¼" (5.7cm)
Each was produced in a limited edition of 250

Tiger Flower

Lion Flower

Glynn Boyd Harte's
Pelargonium was issued as a
framed plaque in 1992.
Height 5⅞" (14.9cm)
Limited edition of 125

Viola Tricolor, a design by
Glynn Boyd Harte
for a box issued in 1992.
Height 2⅛" (5.4cm)

Cheetah Flower

Indian Garden by Joanna Veevers, a
student at the RCA, who won first prize.
Diameter 2¼" (5.7cm)
Limited edition of 250

In 1984 Halcyon Days Enamels organised a competition
in association with *House & Garden* magazine, the
Royal College of Art and The Design Council. The
winners were selected by a panel of judges including
Olive Sullivan, decoration editor (1956-1986) of
House & Garden magazine; the Marquess of
Queensberry, Professor of Ceramics (1959-83)
at the Royal College of Art; and sculptor
Sir Eduardo Paolozzi RA.

Feathers, by Victoria Clarke, a student at
Brighton College of Art, who came second.
Length 2¼" (5.7cm)
Limited edition of 250

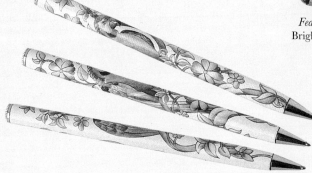

Susan Edwards, formerly a student at
Leicester Polytechnic, was awarded third
prize for this design of parrots
for a ball-point pen.
Length 5" (12.7cm.)

This box with gold and platinum letters was the
result of a design competition held at the Royal
College of Art to mark its 150th anniversary in 1987.
It was won by Clara Hoad, a second-year student in
the department of metalwork and jewellery.
Length 2¼" (5.7cm) Limited edition of 150

Graham Rust's murals and ceiling paintings have brought him international fame.
The most spectacular of these, at Ragley Hall, Warwickshire, took over a decade to complete.
His work has been exhibited world-wide and he has written and illustrated several highly
acclaimed books. He painted the pictures *Cheetah* and *Leopard*
in 1991 especially for this pair of enamel plaques.
Height 10¼" (26cm) Limited edition of 25 pairs

Part of a collection for the Victoria and Albert Museum,
London, based on an original 19th-century textile
design in the Museum's archives.
Height of frame 4¼" (10.8cm)

MUSEUMS & GALLERIES

ART TREASURES from all over the world and from many periods in history have inspired special designs. Royalties are paid to the institutions that have co-operated with Halcyon Days Enamels to produce the objects illustrated here.

Enamels issued in association with
The British Museum, London

Designs inspired by collages by Mrs Delany, which she called 'paper mosaicks'. She was a friend of George III.

The flower motifs on this box are replicas of the enamel panels in a 17th-century necklace in the Hull Grundy Collection.
Diameter 1¾" (4.5cm)

Height of clock 4" (10.2cm)

DESIGN INSPIRED BY
AN IZNIK TILE (1560 – 1580)
IN THE BRITISH MUSEUM,
MADE FOR ONE OF THE
IMPERIAL BUILDINGS
OF ISTANBUL

Design after painted peaches and blossom on a mid-18th-century Qianlong porcelain vase.
Diameter 2¼" (5.7cm)

A box produced in 1988 to mark the 'Süleyman the Magnificent' exhibition at the Museum.
Length 2⅛" (5.4cm)
Limited edition of 500

96

Enamels issued in association with
The Wallace Collection, London

A group of 24ct. gold-encrusted enamels
after the decoration on a Sèvres
18th-century *service de toilette*.

Height of clock 3¼" (8.3cm)

Design based on an 18th-century
Sèvres porcelain plaque.
Length 2¾" (7cm)

The design for this small box
was inspired by a large
18th-century Sèvres
porcelain *pot-pourri* vase.
Length 2" (5cm)

Enamels issued in association with
**The Victoria and Albert Museum,
London**

A design after a 19th-century
printed cotton textile.
Diameter 1⅝" (4cm)

Photograph frame and clock based on a
Victorian printed cotton textile.
Height of clock 2½" (6.4cm)

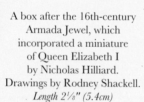

A box after the 16th-century
Armada Jewel, which
incorporated a miniature
of Queen Elizabeth I
by Nicholas Hilliard.
Drawings by Rodney Shackell.
Length 2⅛" (5.4cm)

Two replicas of 18th-century
Bilston enamel boxes in the
Museum's collection.
Oval box length 2⅛" (5.4cm)

The Burrell Collection, Glasgow

A cockerel, after a 1st-century BC mosaic.

A design inspired by an Elizabethan embroidered jacket dating from c.1600-25.
Diameter 1⅝" (4cm)

The Ashmolean Museum, Oxford

Below: An impression of the famous 9th-century Alfred Jewel. The box was produced in 1983 to celebrate the Museum's tercentenary. Drawings by Michael Elleswei.
Length 2⅛" (5.4cm)
Limited edition of 300

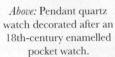

Above: Pendant quartz watch decorated after an 18th-century enamelled pocket watch.

The Fitzwilliam Museum, Cambridge

Design after 'The Billiards Fan', Venice, c.1730. Drawings by Rodney Shackell.
Length 2⅜" (6cm)

A box after *pietra dura* panels of c.1700 that are incorporated into the Fitzwilliam Coin Cabinet, exhibited at the Ashmolean Museum.
Length 2¼" (5.7cm)

99

The Royal Pavilion, Brighton
The Chinese Bridal Procession, after a mural
of c.1818 in the Banqueting Room.
The box was produced in 1991.
Length 2⅞" (7.3cm)
Limited edition of 250

The National Gallery, London
To celebrate the Gallery's 150th
anniversary in 1988, a design
depicting the famous Barry Rooms.
Drawings by Rodney Shackell.
Diameter 1¾" (4.5cm)
Limited edition of 300

**Bantock House Museum,
Wolverhampton**
Replica of a Bilston
enamel box of c.1790.
Length 2⅛" (5.4cm)

**Natural History Museum,
London**
A beaker produced in 1989
based on Edward Lear's book
*Illustrations of the Family Psittacidae
or Parrots*, published 1830-32.
Height 3⅝" (9.3cm)
Limited edition of 500

**The Theatre Museum,
Covent Garden, London**
A box to mark the Museum's
opening in 1987 depicts the
18th-century actor, David Garrick.
Length 2⅜" (6cm)
Limited edition of 250

**The American Museum in Britain,
Claverton Manor, Bath**
Produced in 1981 to celebrate
the Museum's 20th anniversary.
Drawing by Michael Elleswei.
Diameter 2¼" (5.7cm)

Los Angeles County Museum
Birds and fruit within formal borders
– a design based on the *pietra dura*
panels of a magnificent 17th-century
cabinet in the Museum's collection.
Length 2¾" (7cm)

**The Smithsonian Institution,
Washington DC**
The original teddy bear, named
after Theodore Roosevelt.
Diameter 1¼" (3.2cm)

**The Royal Academy of Arts,
London**
To mark the 1987 'Age of Chivalry'
exhibition, a design based on the crown
worn by Princess Blanche, the daughter
of Henry IV, on her marriage in 1401.
Diameter 1¾" (4.5cm)
Limited edition of 200

**The Winterthur Museum,
Delaware**
'Point-to-Point', after a vignette on a
Chinese export porcelain bowl of c.1780.
Length 2¾" (7cm)

PORTRAYALS OF FAMOUS 18th-century Americans exist on rare Georgian enamels; today museums and artistic organisations in the United States commission Halcyon Days to produce designs for enamels that relate to the nation's history.

To mark the bicentenary in 1976 of the American Declaration of Independence, the famous Liberty Bell. Drawing by Frederick Baylis.
Length 1⅞" (4.8cm)
Limited edition of 250

John Hancock, President of Congress, and the facsimiles of all 57 signatories to the Declaration decorate this box commemorating the 1976 bicentenary. Drawing by Ian Adam.
Length 2¾" (7cm)
Limited edition of 500

The bicentenary of the signing of the Treaty of Paris, which ended the American War of Independence (1775-83), was commemorated with this box in 1983. George Washington is shown accepting the British surrender. Drawings by Rodney Shackell.
Diameter 2¼" (5.7cm)
Limited edition of 500

In 1793 George Washington, first President of the USA, laid the cornerstone of the Capitol, Washington DC. This box was produced in 1993 to mark the bicentenary. Drawing by Patricia Chitolie.
Diameter 2⅛" (5.4cm)

A prized exhibit at the
American Museum in Britain is
a 19th-century weather vane
in the form of an American Indian;
its reverse is depicted inside the box.
Length 2⅛" (5.4cm)

The Pennsylvania box of 1994
commemorated the birth of William Penn
in London in 1644. He founded the
state of Pennsylvania in 1682.
Drawings by Rodney Shackell.
Diameter 2¼" (5.7cm)
Limited edition of 350

To commemorate the bicentenary
in 1987 of the American
Constitution, a box bearing the
portraits of George Washington,
the first President, and
James Madison, the fourth.
Drawings by Rodney Shackell.
Diameter 1¾" (4.5cm)

The 20th anniversary in 1989 of the
historic landing of The Apollo II lunar
module prompted The Smithsonian
Institution to commission this box.
Drawing by Ceri Evans.
Diameter 2¼" (5.7cm)

The American War of Independence box
is part of a military history series which is
shown in full on pages 106 and 107.
Diameter 2¼" (5.7cm)
Limited edition of 300

HISTORICAL SUBJECTS

FAMOUS PEOPLE and significant events decorated enamels made in the 18th century; today Halcyon Days Enamels follows this tradition.

The 50th Anniversary in 1990 of the Battle of Britain. The design is based on the plotting clock used in operations rooms at RAF fighter stations. The RAF Benevolent Fund benefited from sales. Drawings by Rodney Shackell. *Diameter 2¼" (5.7cm) Limited edition of 1000*

The Churchill centenary box, issued in 1974. Around the sides are scenes of Blenheim Palace, Chartwell, Admiralty Arch and 10 Downing Street. Drawings by Eric Thomas. *Length 2¾" (7cm) Limited edition of 500*

The 50th anniversary of VE Day, 8th May 1945. Drawing by Christopher Quaile. *Length 2⅛" (5.4cm)*

The 50th anniversary of the landings by allied forces on the Normandy beaches on D-Day, 6th June 1944. Drawing by Frederick Baylis. *Length 2⅛" (5.4cm) Limited edition of 750*

This box was issued in 1989 to mark
The Rt Hon Margaret Thatcher's tenth
anniversary as Prime Minister.
Drawings by Christopher Quaile.
Length 2¾" (7cm)
Limited edition of 500

The Falklands Box, issued in 1982
to support the South Atlantic Fund
and to mark an outstanding
moment in Britain's history.
Drawing by Frederick Baylis.
Length 2⅛" (5.4cm)

The 750th anniversary in 1995
of Westminster Abbey, erected
from 1245 by Henry III.
The Great Seal of Edward
The Confessor appears on the lid.
Drawing by Rodney Shackell.
Diameter 2⅛" (5.4cm)
Limited edition of 250

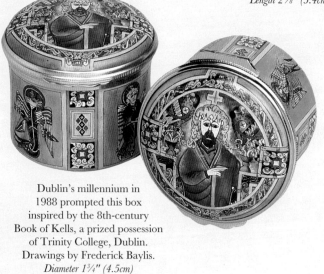

Dublin's millennium in
1988 prompted this box
inspired by the 8th-century
Book of Kells, a prized possession
of Trinity College, Dublin.
Drawings by Frederick Baylis.
Diameter 1¾" (4.5cm)
Limited edition of 100

To mark the 900th anniversary
of the Domesday Book, compiled
in 1086, a box decorated with
scenes from the 11th-century
Bayeux Tapestry.
Drawings by Frederick Baylis.
Diameter 1¾" (4.5cm)

Two boxes from a collection of five to mark
Maritime England Year in 1982,
decorated with historic naval battles.
A brief résumé of the battle and the
coat-of-arms of the reigning monarch
appear inside each box.
The National Maritime Museum, Greenwich,
supplied reference material for the designs.
Drawings by Rodney Shackell.
Length 2¾" (7cm)

The National Maritime Museum, Greenwich,
commissioned this box to commemorate
the quatercentenary of the Spanish Armada
in 1588. The lid design is based on a
16th-century painting in the
Museum's collection.
Drawings by Rodney Shackell.
Length 2¼" (5.7cm)
Limited edition of 500

See description on facing page.

"In a word, Sir,
the gallantry and conduct of
the officers, as well as the bravery of
the soldiers, deserve the highest praise."
Major-General Howe,
Battle of Bunker's Hill,
June 17, 1775.

Milestones in British military
history were recorded with
a collection of six drum-shaped
boxes issued during 1980.
The American War of
Independence box is also
illustrated, closed, on page 103.
The drawings are by David
Rowlands, resident artist at the
National Army Museum.
Diameter 2¼" (5.7cm)
Limited editions, each of 300

The National Maritime
Museum, Greenwich,
commissioned two designs
in 1990 based on English
18th-century enamels
in its collection.

Above: Admiral Lord Nelson
and the message he
signalled at the Battle of
Trafalgar in 1805.
Diameter 1⅜" (4 cm)

Below: HMS Victory,
Lord Nelson's flagship,
launched in 1765.
Length 2⅛" (5.4cm)

'In fourteen hundred and
ninety-two Columbus sailed
the ocean blue...'. The 500th
anniversary in 1992 of
Columbus's discovery
of the New World was
marked with this box.
Drawings and calligraphy
by Frederick Baylis.
Diameter 2¼" (5.7cm)
Limited edition of 500

The Penny Black. The 150th anniversary of the
world's first adhesive postage stamp, issued in 1840.
Calligraphy by Frederick Baylis.
Length 2⅜" (6cm)
Limited edition of 300

A globe-shaped box was
also produced for the
Columbus quincentenary.
Drawings and calligraphy
by Frederick Baylis.
Diameter 2¼" (5.7cm)
Limited edition of 500

In 1192 the Third Crusade ended with a treaty between
Saladin, Sultan of Egypt and Syria, and Richard I of England.
This box marked the 800th anniversary.
Drawings by Christopher Quaile.
Diameter 1¾" (4.5cm) Limited edition of 300

Halley's Comet, named after
the English astronomer,
Edmund Halley (1656-1742),
appears every 75 to 78 years.
This box marked its sighting in 1986.
Drawings by Frederick Baylis.
Diameter 1¾" (4.5cm)

To commemorate the tercentenary in 1988 of the Green Howards regiment, a replica of an enamelled gold snuff box presented by Napoleon to Marshal Ney and left behind in his carriage at Waterloo; it was found by an English officer who gave it to his son, an officer in the Green Howards. Portrait by Rodney Shackell.
Diameter 2¾" (7cm)
Limited edition of 250

A box produced to commemorate the bicentenary of the French Declaration of the Rights of Man in 1789. Drawings by Christopher Quaile.
Diameter 2¼" (5.7cm)

To mark the centenary of Gustave Eiffel's Tower, the centrepiece of the Paris Exhibition of 1889. Drawings by Rodney Shackell.
Length 2⅛" (5.4cm)
Limited edition of 500

To mark the 500th anniversary in 1991 of the birth of Henry VIII. Nine members of his family, including his three children who succeeded him, are depicted on the sides. Drawings by Rodney Shackell.
Diameter 1¾" (4.5cm)
Limited edition of 500

To commemorate the tercentenary of the Glorious Revolution of 1688. Drawings by Rodney Shackell.
Length 2⅜"(6cm)
Limited edition of 300

The bicentenary of the European settlement of Australia from 1788. The flowers represent the seven states and six geographical regions of the country.
Drawings by Ceri Evans.
Diameter 1¾" (4.5cm)
Limited edition of 200

The limited edition for Australia's bicentenary sold out within days, and in response to requests from collectors we produced a second box for the occasion.
Drawings by Ceri Evans.
Length 2⅛" (5.4cm)

A design based on a tiled panel at Membland Hall, Devon, to mark the 150th anniversary in 1984 of William Morris's birth.
Diameter 2¼" (5.7cm)
Limited edition of 500

In 1990 New Zealand's 150th anniversary box commemorated the Treaty of Waitangi between the British Government and the Maori chiefs, and the founding of Wellington and Auckland, all of which took place in 1840.
Drawings by Ceri Evans.
Diameter 1¾" (4.5cm)
Limited edition of 500

The 150th anniversary of Gertrude Jekyll's birth in 1843. A spill vase depicting two of her famous gardens.
Drawings by James Ferguson.
Height 3⅜" (8.5cm) Limited edition of 50

Two boxes produced in 1989: Blanchard's balloon making the
first aerial Channel crossing from Dover to Guines in 1785, and
the Captain of the Society of Goffers at the Royal Blackheath
Golf Club, after a 1778 painting by Lemuel Francis Abbott.
Diameter of each box 2¼" (5.7cm)

LITERARY EDITIONS

QUOTATIONS FROM THE WORKS of famous authors and poets give special pleasure when inscribed on enamels, and literary references have inspired designs for many boxes.

The first commemorative enamel box produced for Halcyon Days in the spring of 1970.
Diameter 1⅝" (4cm)

The Romantic Box was produced in 1972. Inside the lid are lines from Tennyson's *The Daydream:*
'And on her lover's arm she leant,
And round her waist she felt it fold,
And far across the hills they went
in that new world which is the old'.
Drawings by Moira Hoddell.
Length 2¾" (7cm) Limited edition of 500

The bicentenary of Jane Austen's birth was celebrated in 1975 with this box featuring her birthplace, Steventon Rectory; views of Chawton Cottage where she wrote; and the house in College Street, Winchester, where she died.
Drawings by Ian Adam.
Length 2¾" (7cm) Limited edition of 500

The bicentenary of the births of
Jacob Grimm in 1785 and his
brother Wilhelm in 1786.
The box depicts characters
from their stories.
Drawings by Barbara Brown.
Diameter 1¾" (4.5cm)
Limited edition of 750

Sir Arthur Conan Doyle's
Sherlock Holmes stories were first
published in *The Strand Magazine*
in 1891. To celebrate the centenary
this box shows Holmes and Watson
discussing the *Silver Blaze* case
in a railway carriage.
Drawing by Rodney Shackell,
after a *Strand Magazine* illustration.
Diameter 2¼" (5.7cm)
Limited edition of 250

The Vauxhall Gardens box in 1978
depicts lovers enjoying Georgian society's
favourite pleasure ground. Inside the
box is a quotation from Shelley:
'Are we not formed, as notes of music are,
for one another, though dissimilar'.
Drawings by Moira Hoddell.
Length 2¾" (7cm)
Limited edition of 1,000

The Lover's Box, produced in 1981, was
inspired by Elizabeth Barrett Browning's lines:
'If thou must love me, let it be for
naught except for love's sake only'.
Drawings by Moira Hoddell.
Length 2¾" (7cm) Limited edition of 1,000

The 600th anniversary of Chaucer's
The Canterbury Tales was celebrated in 1987 with a
box decorated with scenes based on William Blake's
evocation of the Canterbury Pilgrims, painted in 1810.
Drawings by Rodney Shackell.
Diameter 1¾" (4.5cm) Limited edition of 600

113

THE WRITTEN WORD

THESE SPECIAL EDITIONS record notable historic anniversaries in the world of print,
including those of a distinguished magazine, a famous book of reference
and some of the world's great international newspapers.

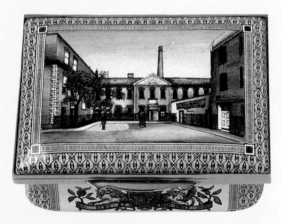

Commissioned by *The Times* to celebrate its bicentenary in
1985, this box shows the original *Times* building
in Printing House Square, after an oil painting in the
newspaper's collection; around the sides are inscriptions
referring to aspects of the newspaper's history.
Drawings by Rodney Shackell.
Length 2⅞" (7.3cm) Limited edition of 200

A box commissioned in 1992
by *Express Newspapers* for a
special presentation.
Length 2⅛" (5.4cm)

A second box, commissioned
by *The Times* in 1985, is
decorated with its
familiar crest and an
outstanding item of
news from each of the
20 decades since the
newspaper was founded.
Drawings by
Michael Elleswei.
Diameter 2¼" (5.7cm)

The centenary of the *Oxford English
Dictionary*, 1984. The definitions of
'Halcyon' and its derivatives are on the
lid, and 'Dictionary' is defined inside.
Length 2⅞" (7.3cm) Limited edition of 350

The New York Times commissioned
this box in 1985. The newspaper's
famous office building is represented on
the lid, while the sides feature:
the 1863 *Decree of Emancipation*,
the Lindbergh flight to Paris
in 1927, VE Day in 1945 and the
moon landing in 1969.
Diameter 2¼" (5.7cm)

A box commissioned in 1982
by *The Illustrated London News*
featuring a Beefeater and
the magazine's logo.
Length 2⅛" (5.4 cm)
Limited edition of 200

A box commissioned in 1976 by the
National Magazine Company,
publishers of *The Connoisseur*, to mark
the magazine's 75th anniversary.
The lid shows the first cover dated
September 1901, designed by
John Byam Shaw, while on the sides
are his vignettes which headed
regular monthly features.
Drawings by Frederick Baylis.
Length 2⅞" (7.3cm)
Limited edition of 250

For *The Financial Times* centenary
we prepared two designs. The one
selected was the circular box featuring
Bracken House, the headquarters at
the time of the centenary in 1988; the
other showed their original building
in Coleman Street, London EC2.
Diameter of round box 2¼" (5.7cm),
Limited edition of 500

ENGLAND'S HERITAGE

THE FINEST GEORGIAN ENAMELS often bore views of classical ruins, Italianate vistas or buildings of local interest. They were the inspiration for the designs in this series, some of which commemorate anniversaries of well-known landmarks.

The centenary in 1995 of The National Trust. This box depicts the 14th-century Clergy House at Alfriston, East Sussex, the first building acquired by the Trust in 1896. Drawing by Rodney Shackell.
Length 2⅛" (5.4cm)
Limited edition of 750

Woburn Abbey, a box commissioned in 1970 by The Duke of Bedford.
Diameter 1⅝" (4cm)

Blenheim Palace, a box commissioned in 1971 by The Duke of Malborough.
Diameter 1⅝" (4cm)

Chatsworth House, a box commissioned in 1977 by The Duchess of Devonshire.
Length 2⅛" (5.4cm)

A panoramic view of Oxford's skyline on a spill vase produced in 1987 depicting: the Sheldonian Theatre, the Clarendon Building, All Souls, the Schools Quadrangle, the Radcliffe Camera, the University Church and Christ Church Cathedral.
Height 3⅜" (8.5cm)

A series of five boxes featuring
London's major museums and galleries
was introduced in 1978. The first was the
Victoria & Albert Museum box, which showed
views of Kensington Palace, the Round Pond,
Kynance Mews and Egerton Crescent.
Drawings by Matthew Wright.
Length 2¼" (5.7cm)
Limited edition of 250

The Tate Gallery box of 1980 was the third in
the series and included views of the
Royal Hospital Chelsea, Sloane Square,
Cheyne Walk and Chelsea Boat Yard.
Drawings by Dennis Flanders.
Length 2¼" (5.7cm)
Limited edition of 250

The British Museum box was issued in 1979.
Its views of Bloomsbury included
Bedford Square, Russell Square,
Great Ormond Street and
Sicilian Avenue.
Drawings by Dennis Flanders.
Length 2¼" (5.7cm)
Limited edition of 250

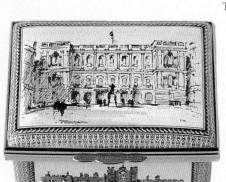

In 1981 the Royal Academy box showed views
of Burlington House, home of the RA,
and local scenes including St James's Palace,
Berkeley Square, Albany, Piccadilly
and the entrance to Green Park.
Drawings by Sir Hugh Casson PRA.
Length 2¼" (5.7cm) Limited edition of 250

To mark the 150th anniversary of the
National Gallery the final box in the series
was issued in 1982 and included views of
Trafalgar Square, Admiralty Arch,
Horse Guards Parade and Cecil Court.
Drawings by Dennis Flanders.
Length 2¼" (5.7cm) Limited edition of 250

A box to support the Appeal Fund for the tercentenary of Rotten Row, built for William III in 1690 as part of a carriage drive between the palaces of Westminster and Kensington. Drawings by Rodney Shackell.
Length 2⅛" (5.4cm) Limited edition of 300

This box marks the 150th anniversary of Nelson's Column in 1990. Drawings by Sarah Tracey.
Length 2⅛" (5.4cm)

The tercentenary of Bond Street in 1985 was commemorated with a box featuring portraits of famous people whose lives were intertwined with the history of the street. St John Ambulance benefited from sales. Drawings by Shirley Curzon.
Diameter 1⅝" (4cm)
Limited edition of 300

In 1688 Mr Edward Lloyd opened a coffee house in Tower Street, London. Lloyd's of London commissioned this commemorative spill vase in 1988. Drawing by Rodney Shackell.
Height 3⅜" (8.5cm) Limited edition of 500

The London clock has capital views on each of its five enamel panels. Drawings by Patricia Chitolie.
Height 2½" (6.4cm)

To mark the visit of The American Bar
Association to Britain, 15th-20th July 1985.
Drawings by Dennis Flanders.
Length 2¼" (5.7cm)
Limited edition of 500

This box marked the 800th
anniversary of the Mayoralty of the
City of London in 1989.
Drawings by Anthony Maynard.
Diameter 2¼" (5.7cm)

The Downing Street box, produced in
1983, showed the Prime Minister's
official residence and views of the
Houses of Parliament, Admiralty Arch
and the Horse Guards Parade.
Drawings by Jason Lewis.
Diameter 2¼" (5.7cm)
Limited edition of 1,000

The Bank of England was founded in 1694 by
Royal Charter and in 1994 this box featured
Sir John Soane's Old Lady of Threadneedle Street.
Drawings by Rodney Shackell.
Length 2¾" (7cm) Limited edition of 300

PLANES & TRAINS & CARS

DESIGNS DEPICTING momentous events in the history of transportation recall the drama and pioneering spirit that lay behind many of the inventions that changed the world.

The 50th anniversary of Amy Johnson's 1930 solo flight to Australia.
Drawings by Ian Adam.
Diameter 1⅝" (4cm)
Limited edition of 300

In 1903 Wilbur and Orville Wright made the first powered aeroplane flight. The 75th anniversary box shows their Flyer 1 and other early aircraft.
Drawings by Ian Adam.
Diameter 2¼" (5.7cm)
Limited edition of 250

The 75th anniversary in 1987 of the Royal Air Force.
Drawings by Rodney Shackell.
Diameter 2¼" (5.7cm)
Limited edition of 250

The 150th anniversary of the first railway passenger service in 1830, between Liverpool and Manchester, was marked with two editions.
Drawings by Rodney Shackell.
Length 2¾" (7cm)
Limited editions, each of 150

To commemorate the 60th Anniversary of
the 1923 Railways Act, the star locomotives
of the four divisions inaugurated by
the Act are depicted on these boxes.
Drawings by Rodney Shackell.
Length 2⅛" (5.4cm)

To mark the centenary of the motor car in 1986 a box
decorated with the first Daimler and the first Benz, both
patented in 1886. The edition was issued in association with
Lord Montagu of Beaulieu's National Motor Museum.
Drawings by Michael Elleswei.
Length 2⅞" (7.3cm) Limited edition of 500

For the 75th anniversary of the first Rolls Royce this box,
produced in 1979, features the 1911 Silver Ghost Ceremonial
Phaeton built for the Maharajah of Mysore. A parallel
American edition of boxes was issued by the James C Leake
Collection in Muskogee, Oklahoma. Drawings by Ian Adam.
Length 2⅞" (7.3cm)
Limited editions of 500 (UK) and 500 (USA)

THE SPORTING LIFE

IN THE 18th and 19th centuries sporting events were among the most popular of subjects for artists and engravers; similar themes feature in many editions we produce today.

The 150th anniversary in 1979 of the first University Boat Race. Cambridge blue and Oxford blue versions were produced. Drawings by David Rowlands.
Length 2¾" (7cm)

The Wimbledon centenary box with a scene depicting the first Men's Singles in 1877. Drawing by Ian Adam.
Diameter 2¼" (5.7cm)

To commemorate the bicentenary of the Marylebone Cricket Club, founded in 1787 by the legendary Thomas Lord. Drawings by Rodney Shackell.
Length 2⅛" (5.4cm)

To mark the centenary of The Cyclists' Touring Club, formed in 1878 to 'help tourists secure companions'. Drawing by Ian Adam.
Height 3⅝" (9.2cm)
Limited edition of 350

To mark the opening in 1993 of a Halcyon Days shop in The Gleneagles Hotel, Scotland. Drawings by Patricia Chitolie.
Diameter 2¾" (7cm)

122

Two boxes issued in 1983 and 1984 celebrated famous
Derby winners: *Hyperion* in 1933 and *Nijinsky* in 1970.
Drawings by David Astin.
Diameter 2¼" (5.7cm) Limited editions, each of 500

To commemorate the bicentenary of the Derby in
1980, the Prince of Wales, later Edward VII, is shown
leading in his 1896 Derby winner, *Persimmon*.
Vignettes of other Derby winners appear on the sides.
Drawings by Moira Hoddell.
Length 2⅞" (7.3cm) Limited edition of 200

The Grand National was first held
at Aintree in 1839 and to celebrate
its 150th anniversary this box was
produced showing the first winner,
Mr Elmore's *Lottery*.
Drawings by Rodney Shackell.
Length 2¾" (7cm)
Limited edition of 500

WILDLIFE

THE WORLD WILDLIFE Collection, issued in 1973 in association with the WWF, was the first of many designs produced throughout the years to support organisations involved in conservation.

A World Wildlife UK edition of 350 sets was distributed by Halcyon Days, and a USA edition, also of 350, was distributed by Cartier, New York. Drawings by Caroline Ebborn.

Snow Leopard

Bald Eagle

Polar Bear

Galapagos Penguin

Hawaiian Goose

Diameter of round boxes 2¼" (5.7cm)
Length of oval boxes 2¾" (7cm)

The Audubon Collection, made in 1980, was a trio of boxes reproducing in miniature illustrations from Jean-Jacques Audubon's *The Birds of America* (1827-1838). The collection commemorated the 75th anniversary of the National Audubon Society, USA, which benefited from sales. Issued by Halcyon Days in the UK and the Horchow Collection, Dallas, in the USA. Drawings by Shireen Faircloth.
Length 2¾" (7cm)
Limited editions of 150 in the UK and the USA

A famous African elephant named Ahmed was Kenya's National Monument – before it was shot. It is depicted on the embossed lid of a box after a painting by the artist Fleur Cowles.
Length 2⅞" (7.3cm)
Limited edition of 200

Ruffed Grouse

Key West Quail-dove

Bald Eagle

The Ceylon Elephant was the sixth in the World Wildlife Collection, featured on the facing page.

125

BONBONNIERES

ENAMEL BONBONNIERES are among the most valuable of all antique English enamels. The contemporary examples illustrated here presented a challenge to the manufacturers in Bilston who have so skilfully created this amusing collection.

A bullfrog.
Diameter 1¾" (4.5cm)

Apple, pear
and cherry.
*Diameter of apple
1⅝" (4cm)*

Fox with cubs.
Diameter 1⅝" (4cm)

Saddleback pig.
Length 2⅛" (5.4cm)

Giant panda with bamboo.
Height 2½" (6.3cm)

Replica of an
18th-century *bonbonnière*.
Diameter 1⅝" (4cm)

Indian elephant.
Length 1⅝" (4cm)

Recumbent tiger.
Length 2¾" (7cm)

The head of a jaguar.
Length 1¾" (4.5cm)

Mandarin duck.
Length 2⅛" (5.4cm)

Wild rabbit.
Length 2⅛" (5.4cm)

Cabbage Rose.
Diameter 1¼" (3.2cm)

THE COLLECTORS' CIRCLE was established in 1983 especially for those who had previously bought Halcyon Days Enamels' limited editions. The first two designs depicted subjects that were among the most beautiful and famous to be found on antique English enamels.

Miniature clock with scenes after
Watteau paintings.
Drawings by Jason Lewis.
Width 2¾" (7cm)
Limited edition of 200

Birds with an Overturned Basket of Fruit
by the artist-engraver Robert Hancock
(c.1730-1817), issued in 1983.
Drawings by Rodney Shackell.
Length 2⅛" (5.4cm)
Limited edition of 500

To commemorate the tercentenary of
Jean Antoine Watteau's birth in 1684,
a box inspired by his designs
for *The Four Seasons*.
Drawings by Rodney Shackell.
Length 2¼" (5.7cm)
Limited edition of 300

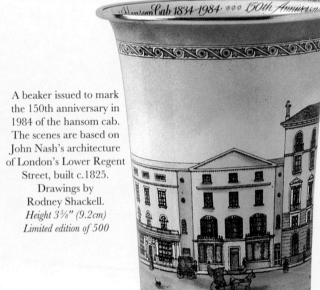

A beaker issued to mark
the 150th anniversary in
1984 of the hansom cab.
The scenes are based on
John Nash's architecture
of London's Lower Regent
Street, built c.1825.
Drawings by
Rodney Shackell.
Height 3⅜" (9.2cm)
Limited edition of 500

In 1985 the City of Wolverhampton
celebrated its millenary and J M W Turner's
1795 view of St Peter's Church from
High Green, now Queen Square,
was chosen for this special box.
Drawing by Rodney Shackell.
Length 2¼" (5.7cm)
Limited edition of 300

In 1987 the anniversaries of
Queen Victoria's accession in 1837
and her Golden Jubilee in 1887 were
commemorated with this box.
Portraits by Shirley Curzon.
Diameter 2¼" (5.7cm)
Limited edition of 300

A scene from Hogarth's
A Rake's Progress, painted in 1735.
This box marked the paintings'
250th anniversary in 1985.
Drawings by
Rodney Shackell.
Length 2" (5cm)
Limited edition of 250

A replica of an 18th-century English
enamel box depicting *The Haymakers*
by Robert Hancock.
Drawing by Rodney Shackell.
Length 2¾" (7cm) Limited edition of 300

This tribute to
Lord Byron (1788-1824), was
issued in 1988, the bicentenary of his birth.
Drawings by Rodney Shackell.
Length 2¾" (7cm) Limited edition of 200

A famous Robert Hancock design, *The Tea Party*, decorates this 1989 box and was also featured on one of our 25th anniversary editions, shown on page 144. Drawings by Rodney Shackell.
Length 2⅛" (5.4cm)
Limited edition of 500

The 150th anniversary of the birth of Paul Cézanne (1839-1906) prompted this 1988 box reproducing an early view of Mont Sainte Victoire.
Length 2¼" (5.7cm) Limited edition of 100

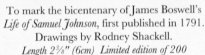

To mark the bicentenary of James Boswell's *Life of Samuel Johnson*, first published in 1791. Drawings by Rodney Shackell.
Length 2⅜" (6cm) Limited edition of 200

The 800th anniversary in 1989 of the crowning of King Richard I of England – Richard Coeur de Lion. Drawings by Christopher Quaile.
Diameter 1¾" (4.5cm) Limited edition of 500

The Parisian dancer, Jane Avril, one of Toulouse-Lautrec's most enduring images, was the subject of a Collectors' Circle box of 1989.
Length 2⅜" (6cm) Limited edition of 200

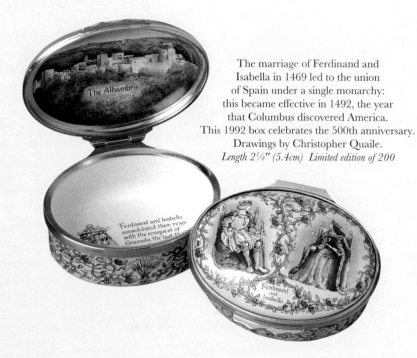

The marriage of Ferdinand and
Isabella in 1469 led to the union
of Spain under a single monarchy:
this became effective in 1492, the year
that Columbus discovered America.
This 1992 box celebrates the 500th anniversary.
Drawings by Christopher Quaile.
Length 2⅛" (5.4cm) Limited edition of 200

In 1991 the fourth in our series of
designs after Robert Hancock shows a
River Scene with Swans.
Drawings by Rodney Shackell.
Length 2⅛" (5.4cm)
Limited edition of 500

The centenary in 1992 of the first
performance of Oscar Wilde's
Lady Windermere's Fan.
Drawing by Shirley Curzon.
Length 2⅜" (6cm)
Limited edition of 200

The 450th anniversary in 1992 of Mary
Queen of Scots' accession to the throne of
Scotland when she was less than a week old.
Drawings by Christopher Quaile.
Length 2⅜" (6cm)
Limited edition of 200

The 900th anniversary of the founding of Durham Cathedral
was commemorated in 1993. The cathedral, thought to be the
most beautiful in England, was built as a shrine to St Cuthbert
of Lindisfarne, the 7th-century monk and missionary.
Drawings by Christopher Quaile.
Diameter 2⅛" (5.4cm) Limited edition of 250

Sarah Bernhardt is portrayed
on a box commemorating the
150th anniversary of the legendary
actress's birth in 1844.
The image is after a poster
by Alphonse Mucha.
Drawings by Shirley Curzon.
Length 2⅛" (5.4cm)
Limited edition of 150

In 1992 this plaque was produced illustrating
Jean de La Fontaine's fable of *The Cock and the Fox*.
Drawing by Rodney Shackell.
Height 4⅛" (10.5cm) Limited edition of 100

A second plaque produced in 1993 illustrates
La Fontaine's fable of *The Hare and the Frogs*.
Drawing by Rodney Shackell.
Height 4⅛" (10.5cm) Limited edition of 100

Two specially commissioned boxes produced in 1988: the headquarters
of Tarmac plc, and a design produced for the Master of the
Worshipful Company of Saddlers in the City of London.
Length of oval 2¾" (7cm)

CHARITABLE CAUSES

FROM THE EARLY 1970s special Halcyon Days Enamels designs have been produced in association with many British and international charities; donations are made to the relevant organisations on all sales of these editions.

The St Paul's box, issued in aid of the St Paul's Cathedral Appeal in 1971, was presented at The Mansion House to Queen Elizabeth The Queen Mother by the Lord Mayor, Sir Peter Studd. Drawing by Geoffrey Fletcher.
Diameter 2¼" (5.7cm)
Limited edition of 100

A box produced for MENCAP in 1984 featured a sketch of the young Queen Victoria on horseback, after the painting by Landseer which hangs in Clarence House, home of Queen Elizabeth The Queen Mother, the charity's Patron. Drawing by Ian Adam.
Length 2⅜" (6cm)
Limited edition of 500

St John Ambulance's centenary was marked in 1977 with this box emblazoned with a Maltese cross.
Diameter 1⅜" (4cm)

In 1982, to support the Mary Rose Project, this box was produced featuring Henry VIII's famous ship. The drawing by Rodney Shackell is after a picture in a list known as the Anthony Rolls, completed in 1546.
Length 2¼" (5.7cm) Limited edition of 350

This 1982 box commemorates the tercentenary of the foundation of the Royal Hospital Chelsea by Charles II in 1682. The design is based on the Hospital's own ceremonial drum, with an 18th-century view of Wren's famous building from across the Thames. Drawings by Rodney Shackell.
Diameter 2¼" (5.7cm)
Limited edition of 500

The Save the Children Fund's special appeal for the children of East Africa prompted this box, produced in 1985.
Drawings by Barbara Brown.
Length 2⅛" (5.4cm)

A watercolour of Algernon Swinburne and his sisters, painted in 1843 by George Richmond, was graciously chosen by The Princess Margaret as a subject for a box to mark her forty years as Patron of Dr Barnardo's (1945-1985).
Length 2⅛" (5.4cm)
Limited edition of 250

A view of Geneva, after an early 19th-century engraving, decorates a box produced in 1984 for the 120th anniversary of the First Geneva Convention in 1864, issued to support the British Red Cross Society.
Drawing by Rodney Shackell.
Length 2⅛" (5.4cm)

The Queen's corgis, reproduced by gracious permission of Her Majesty from a drawing by Raphael Maklouf. Issued in support of the Animal Health Trust of which she is Patron.
Diameter 1⅝" (4cm)

The centenary, in 1984, of the NSPCC was commemorated with a box depicting the Sitwell children playing on a rocking horse, after a watercolour by the 19th-century artist Octavia Oakley. By kind permission of Sir Reresby Sitwell.
Drawing by Eric Thomas.
Length 2⅛" (5.4cm)
Limited edition of 250

For the 60th anniversary of British Red Cross Youth, founded in 1924, a box depicting Highgrove, home of The Prince and Princess of Wales; The Princess is the charity's Patron.
Drawing by Felix Kelly.
Length 2¼" (5.7cm) Limited edition of 250

Sir James Barrie bequeathed the copyright of Peter Pan to
Great Ormond Street Children's Hospital in 1929.
The oval box has drawings by Barbara Brown and the small
box is after an Arthur Rackham 1906 illustration in *Peter Pan in
Kensington Gardens*. From a 1994 collection of enamels produced
in association with the Hospital Fund.

Length 2⅛" (5.4cm)

In 1989 this box was produced
to support the Riding for
the Disabled Association.
Drawing by Frederick Baylis.
Length 2⅛" (5.4cm)
Limited edition of 250

Diameter 1¼" (3.2cm)

Elton John commissioned this box in 1994.
It is after an 18th-century painting
attributed to François Huet (1772-1813)
in his personal collection. A donation
was made to the Elton John AIDS
Foundation for every box sold.
Length 2⅜" (6cm)

A globe-shaped box featuring many
of the world's endangered species
was produced in 1994 in association
with Friends of the Earth.
Drawings by Fiona Powers.
Length 2⅜" (6cm)

A replica in miniature of a 1960 painting
by Claude Harrison of Ben and
Emma Holland-Martin at Bell's Castle,
produced in 1985 to support the NSPCC.
Length 2⅛" (5.4cm)
Limited edition of 250

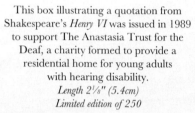

This box illustrating a quotation from Shakespeare's *Henry VI* was issued in 1989 to support The Anastasia Trust for the Deaf, a charity formed to provide a residential home for young adults with hearing disability.
Length 2⅛" (5.4cm)
Limited edition of 250

This 1990 box featuring famous 19th-century actors was produced for SOS, the Stars' Organisation for Spastics. The design is based on theatrical prints from the collection of Sir John and Lady Mills. Drawings by Shirley Curzon.
Diameter 1⅝" (4cm)

The 900th anniversary of the great 11th-century basilica of San Marco, Venice, is commemorated by this box produced in 1994, the inside of which depicts its famous Bronze Horses and the Lion of San Marco. Venice in Peril benefits from sales. Drawings by Patricia Warner.
Length 2⅜" (6cm)

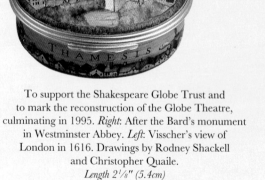

A box to mark the 125th anniversary of the British Red Cross in 1995 depicting Queen Elizabeth The Queen Mother greeting a Red Cross Commandant during a visit to Barnett Hill, Surrey, in 1943. Drawing by Shirley Curzon.
Length 2⅛" (5.4cm)
Limited edition of 500

To support the Shakespeare Globe Trust and to mark the reconstruction of the Globe Theatre, culminating in 1995. *Right*: After the Bard's monument in Westminster Abbey. *Left*: Visscher's view of London in 1616. Drawings by Rodney Shackell and Christopher Quaile.
Length 2⅛" (5.4cm)

THE BROOK STREET COLLECTION was introduced in 1993 as an exclusive group of designs that included replicas of 18th-century English enamels as well as special subjects of particular interest to collectors of Halcyon Days Enamels.

Replica of an 18th-century box.
Length 2⅛" (5.4cm)

A romantic message, typical of the genre, for a design based on an 18th-century Bilston box.
Diameter 1⅝" (4cm)

A *trompe l'oeil* photograph frame inspired by an 18th-century classical portico. Drawing by Rodney Shackell.
Height 4⅝" (11.8cm)

The Halcyon Days Legend.
Diameter 1⅜" (3.5cm)

Replica of an 18th-century egg-shaped box.
Diameter 1¼" (3.2cm)

A replica of a rare London enamel patch box of c.1755; the underside of the box has similar gold-encrusted decoration.
Length 2¾" (7cm)

Kingfisher and Ducks by a River is after an engraving attributed to Robert Hancock (c.1730-1817). Drawing by Pamela Dowson.
Length 2¾" (7cm)

Portraits of Admiral Lord Nelson and Emma, Lady Hamilton, his beloved mistress, are featured on enamel plaques. Lord Nelson, after Lemuel Francis Abbott; Lady Hamilton, after George Romney.
Height of frames 3⅜" (8.5cm)

Replicas of 18th-century Bilston boxes.
Length of oval box 2⅛" (5.4cm)

The romantic inscription on this box was taken from a quotation which John Julius Norwich discovered in The British Museum's copy of Alexander Browne's *The Art of Painting in Miniature* (1669). Lord Norwich included the lines in his 1987 anthology, *Christmas Crackers*.
Drawings by Christopher Quaile.
Length 2⅜" (6cm)

ONE-OF-A-KIND

UNIQUE ENAMELS FOR special occasions can feature almost any subject based on reference material, such as a painting or a photograph. An inscription set within a decorative border is an alternative for a presentation box.

An heraldic crest by
Anthony Phillips.
Diameter 2¼" (5.7cm)

A racehorse by Anne Upson.
Length 2¾" (7cm)

A blue-point
Siamese cat by
Anne Upson.
Diameter 1⅝" (4cm)

Two anniversary boxes,
one with a facsimile of
handwriting.
Diameter of small box 1¼" (3.2cm)

A castle in the Cotswolds by Anthony Phillips.
Length 2⅞" (7.3cm)

SPECIALLY COMMISSIONED

ORGANISATIONS LARGE AND SMALL commission enamels for presentation on special occasions or to mark noteworthy events in their history. Halcyon Days' artists and calligraphers excel at producing these distinctive designs.

The BBC's Antiques Road Show commissioned this box in 1994.
Diameter 1⅝" (4cm)

The Young Presidents Organisation, Canadian University, Toronto, 1981.
Length 2¾" (7cm)

A box was made to celebrate the Coca-Cola Company's centenary in 1986.
Length 2⅛" (5.4cm)

Taylor Joynson Garrett, solicitors, commissioned this box decorated with a facsimile of an 18th-century *Letters of Administration*, to celebrate the London meeting of Interlex in 1980.
Diameter 2¼" (5.7cm)

The Perrier egg-shaped box commissioned for Christmas 1985.
Diameter 1⅝" (4cm)

This box, commissioned to celebrate the 'Encore of The Three Tenors' concert in Los Angeles on 16th July 1994, depicts Carreras, Domingo and Pavarotti with conductor Zubin Mehta.
Length 2⅜" (6cm)

ANNIVERSARY EDITIONS

HALCYON DAYS ENAMELS celebrated the 10th and 15th anniversaries of the revival with the two editions illustrated below. The other enamels shown mark the 25th anniversary and for these the 18th-century custom of basing designs on the works of eminent historic artists has been followed.

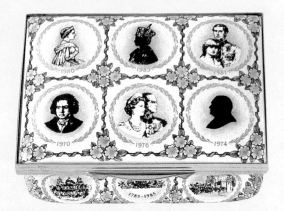

For the 10th anniversary in 1980 a box transfer-printed in the 18th-century manner depicts stages in the processes of enamelling on copper, inspired by engravings in Diderot's famous *Encyclopédie au Dictionnaire raisonné des sciences, des arts et des métiers*, published 1751-65. Drawings by Moira Hoddell.
Length 2¾" (7cm)
Limited edition of 300

To mark the 15th anniversary, a design showing details of outstanding limited editions issued each year from 1970 to 1985.
Length 2⅞" (7.3cm)
Limited edition of 150

A Gallant Offering a Rose decorates a small quartz clock on the reverse of which is pictured *The Haymakers*, after Robert Hancock.
Height 2½" (6.4cm)
Limited edition of 250

Parrot and Fruit after a Robert Hancock engraving.
Diameter 1¼" (3.2cm)

A design inspired by a London enamel of c.1765.
Length 2⅛" (5.4cm)

Painted enamel plaques were much favoured by English 18th-century enamellers and some of the most elegant subjects depicted by them have been chosen to decorate this set of four, produced to celebrate the 25th anniversary.
Width of gilt-brass frames 3" (7.6cm)
Each in a limited edition of 250

Above: *The Haymakers* after
Robert Hancock (c.1730-1817).
Below: *A Gallant Offering a Rose* after an
unattributed 18th-century engraving.

Two famous subjects by the romantic French
artist Jean Antoine Watteau (1684-1721).
Above: *La Cascade*.
Below: *Les Amusements Champêtres*.

The Tea Party was one of
Robert Hancock's most appealing
subjects and it can be found on rare
18th-century ceramics as well as on enamels.
Here it is portrayed against a
diapered background.
Diameter 2⅛" (5.4cm)

An 8-day carriage clock and a box
decorated with *Birds with an Overturned
Basket of Fruit* after an engraving by
Robert Hancock illustrated in
The Ladies Amusement, a book of
designs published c.1760.

Height 5¾" (14.6cm)
Limited edition of 25

Length 2⅜" (6cm)
Limited edition of 250

DESIGN CO-OPERATION

THE ORGANISATIONS listed below have co-operated with Halcyon Days Enamels
and, where appropriate, have provided reference material for designs;
in each instance royalties have been paid on sales.

EUROPE

Amsterdam:	Rijksmuseum
Bath:	American Museum in Britain
Beaulieu:	National Motor Museum
Brighton:	Royal Pavilion
Cambridge:	Fitzwilliam Museum
Dublin:	Trinity College
Edinburgh:	Royal Scottish Museum
Glasgow:	Burrell Collection
Greenwich:	National Maritime Museum
Island of Ischia:	William Walton Foundation
Liverpool:	Lady Lever Art Gallery
London:	British Museum
	D'Oyly Carte Opera Company
	English National Opera
	London Symphony Orchestra
	National Gallery
	Natural History Museum
	Tate Gallery
	Royal Academy of Arts
	Royal Opera House
	Royal Ballet
	Royal College of Art
	Sadler's Wells
	Victoria and Albert Museum
	Wallace Collection
Munich:	Bayerische Verwaltung der Stadtlichen Schlösser, Gärten und Seen
Oxford:	Ashmolean Museum
Stratford upon Avon:	Royal Shakespeare Theatre
Wolverhampton:	Bantock House Museum

UNITED STATES OF AMERICA

Los Angeles:	Los Angeles County Museum
San Francisco:	San Francisco Opera
Winterthur:	Winterthur Museum
Chicago:	Art Institute of Chicago
	Chicago Lyric Opera
New York City:	Cooper-Hewitt Museum
	Lincoln Center
	Metropolitan Museum of Art
	Metropolitan Opera
Toronto:	Royal Ontario Museum
Charlottesville:	University of Virginia Art Museum
Washington DC:	The Smithsonian Institution

CHARITIES

Anastasia Trust for the Deaf
Animal Health Trust
Barnardo's
British Red Cross Society
British Red Cross Youth
Elton John AIDS Foundation
Friends of the Earth
Great Ormond Street Children's Hospital
Mary Rose Project
MENCAP
National Trust
National Society for the Prevention of Cruelty to Children
Riding for the Disabled
Rotten Row 300 Appeal
Royal Society for the Protection of Birds
St John Ambulance
St Paul's Cathedral Appeal
Save the Children Fund
Shakespeare Globe Trust
Soldiers', Sailors' and Airmen's Families Association
Stars Organisation for Spastics
Venice in Peril
World Wildlife Fund

INDEX